VARANASI
A Pilgrimage to Light

By the same author:

Devalaya: Great Temples of India
Devi Devata: Gods & Goddesses of India
Tirtha: Holy Pilgrim Centres of the Hindus
Chaar Dhaam: A Guide to the Hindu Pilgrimages
Badrinath
Dwarka
Puri
Rameshwaram

VARANASI

A Pilgrimage to Light

Subhadra Sen Gupta

Rupa • Co

Copyright © Subhadra Sen Gupta 2004

Published 2004 by
Rupa & Co
7/16, Ansari Road, Daryaganj,
New Delhi 110 002

Sales Centres:
Allahabad Bangalore Chandigarh Chennai
Hyderabad Jaipur Kathmandu Kolkata
Ludhiana Mumbai Pune

All rights reserved.
No part of this publication may be reproduced, stored in a retrieval system, or transmitted, in any form or by any means, electronic, mechanical, photocopying, recording or otherwise, without the prior permission of the publishers.

ISBN 81-291-0165-3

Typeset 11 pts. ClassicalGaramond by
Nikita Overseas Pvt Ltd,
1410 Chiranjiv Tower,
43 Nehru Place
New Delhi 110 019

Printed in India by
Rekha Printers Pvt Ltd,
A-102/1 Okhla Industrial Area,
Phase-II, New Delhi-110 020

*For my aunt and uncle
Krishna and P.K.Gupta
Thank you for introducing me to Kashi.
With love.*

CONTENTS

VARANASI IS A STATE OF MIND	1
OM NAMAH SHIVAYA!	10
UNFORGETTABLE GANGA River of Life and Liberation	32
THE GHATS BY THE GANGA Stairways to Heaven	43
TEMPLES OF VARANASI A City of Shrines	70
HISTORY OF VARANASI Ancient and Still Eternal	102
VARANASI TODAY Mauj and Masti Among the Cows	119
SARNATH Buddham Sharanam Gatchami	132
GLOSSARY	141
BIBLIOGRAPHY	145
INDEX	147

One

VARANASI IS A STATE OF MIND

"*Where the magic of the world is made,*
Where the whole world of moving and non-moving things
Seems the dalliance of the mind,
Is the One Place with the nature of the Supreme Soul Truth,
Luminous Wisdom, and Bliss.
I am that Kashi whose essence is self-knowledge."

—'Five verses on Kashi'—
Adi Shankaracharya, eighth century philosopher

Kashi, Banaras, Varanasi ... whatever you call it, is the most maddeningly elusive city. For centuries writers, poets, painters and fabulists have tried to comprehend its character. But Kashi is not interested in being understood or being categorised. You can show an aspect of it in words or images but seldom feel that you have completely captured its prismatic character. It is a place of pilgrimage like many other tirthas in this land but it is like none other. It is ancient but also oddly vivacious and young. It celebrates life but also has a symbiotic relationship with death. It is cynical, decadent and compassionate, calm and disturbing, passionate and detached. Generous Varanasi gives you what you seek. Wearing its myriad, many-hued masks, it can be anything you want it to be.

First of all, Varanasi is the supreme *tirthasthana*, the greatest place of pilgrimage for Hindus. Any pilgrim sitting on its ghats or carrying flowers into a temple precinct will tell you, reciting this ancient shloka from the *Kashi Khanda*, the list of the Saptapuris, the seven sacred cities,

"*Kashi, Kanchi, Maya, Ayodhya, Avantika
Mathura, Dwaravati chaiva saptaita mokshadayika.*"

Kashi, Kanchipuram, Maya (Haridwar), Ayodhya, Avantika (Ujjain), Mathura and Dwaravati (Dwarka) are the seven cities that offer the liberation of *moksha*.

Varanasi is thrice blessed. It is the earthly home of one of the most worshipped of the Hindu pantheon of gods. It stands by the banks and is sanctified by the waters of the most sacred of India's rivers, Ganga. And finally it has some of the holiest temples in the land. The *Kashi Khanda*, a book of praise of the city, says, "The Ganga river, Lord Shiva, and the city of Kashi make the Trinity of grace and perfect bliss."

Shiva, that volatile, compassionate and complex God and his consort Parvati chose this city as their abode on earth. Ganga, that turbulent, life giving river flows past it with serene majesty, touching its stepped embankments, blessing these *ghats* with its celestial and sacred waters, purifying them and making them eternally holy. And then, through history, people came from all across the country and built *devalayas* and *ashrams*, shrines and hermitages, along this curve of the Ganga that transformed Varanasi-Kashi into the quintessential tirtha.

The Supreme Tirtha

For a Hindu a *tirtha* is a place of pilgrimage and in any list of the greatest *tirthasthanas* of the land the first name is always Varanasi. And this has been so for centuries. A *tirtha* is resonant with three elements that make it so sacred—it is *shuchi*, pure; it brings *punya*, merit and goodness and it is *shubha*, auspicious. The words Kashi and Varanasi have become the symbol of this purity and goodness, so that the *tirtha* of Kanchipuram is called *Dakshina Kashi*, 'the Kashi of the South'. There are places of pilgrimage named after it like Uttara Kashi, the northern Kashi in the hills and Shivakashi in the south.

A *tirtha* is a spiritual goal. The *Skanda Purana* states, "Truth, forgiveness, control of senses, kindness to all living beings and simplicity are also *tirthas*." In the tolerant and life enhancing beliefs of Hinduism, a *tirthasthana* and a *tirthayatra*, are finally a state of mind. You find a *tirthasthana* where you seek it—by the banks of a holy river, at the foot of a mountain, under a sacred tree or even at the feet of a great saint or guru. Kashi is such a state of mind and a symbol for the Hindus. You can find Kashi anywhere. For those on a spiritual quest, their teachers tell them to seek Kashi in their soul.

A tirtha is a spiritual ford. Along the Ganga Kashi is that special place in our lives where we can make the crossing from this mortal life to the liberation that lies beyond. Hindus believe that it is a sacred place where we can let go of the burdens of worldly *samsara* and reach out to the eternal peace of salvation and journey to the heaven they call *swarga*. As the pilgrim will tell you, here you hope to move from the illusory world of *marta* below on 'this shore' to the 'far shore' of *moksha*, the final liberation from this endless cycle of births and deaths. The pilgrims come to Kashi because at this ford it is Lord Shiva himself who will row you across this spiritual river as he recites the Taraka Mantra, the prayer of the divine ferryman into your ears, and the *moksha* that he brings is the purest of all. As Adi Shankaracharya wrote so beautifully,

> "In Kashi the Light shines
> The Light illumines everything
> Whoever knows that Light
> Truly reaches Kashi."

Every devout Hindu dreams of visiting the greatest *tirthas* of the Saptapuris of Varanasi, Kanchipuram, Haridwar, Ayodhya, Mathura, Dwarka and Ujjain. Also the Chaar Dhaams of Badrinath, Dwarka, Puri and Rameshwaram. For most of them the first one they want to visit is Varanasi. It has drawn pilgrims and philosophers, intrigued poets and scholars, mesmerised travellers and artists since the beginning of history. In ancient times no one ever wrote a history of this city but it is mentioned often in the sacred literature of our land. We find Varanasi in the *Ramayana, Mahabharata,* the *Puranas* and the Buddhist *Jataka* tales. Kashi appears in the writings of travellers from Huien Tsang in the seventh century who was on his way to Sarnath to the sixteenth century Italian Jean Baptist Tavernier standing in awe in the sanctum of the Bindu Madhav Temple.

They call this *tirtha* Kashi, the city of light, as it is said to bring enlightenment to people, especially those on a spiritual quest to discover a meaning in their lives. It is also Varanasi, that sacred space between the two rivers Varuna and Asi that flow into the Ganga. It is Avimukta, the city that Shiva never forsakes. It is also Shiva and Parvati's Anandavana, their forest of bliss and Rudravasa, the city of Rudra-Shiva. Finally it is Mahashmashana, the great cremation ground, where Shiva waits for your souls and no death is as liberating as a death in Kashi. The city has been described poetically for its beauty and in ancient texts called *Sudarshana, Surandhana* and *Brahmavardhana*. A city of flowers—Pushpavati and Malini and enchanting—Ramya and Mukulini.

The city is visualised as a traditional *mandala* of concentric circles. The largest circle including the outskirts is Kashi. The second, the area between the Varuna and Asi rivers is Varanasi. The third is Avimukta, the city free of sin, and finally the heart of the *mandala* is the circle around the Kashi Vishwanath temple called *antargriha*, the inner sanctum.

Kashi draws the world to its temple precincts and river ghats. People come here to celebrate their happiness, they come to atone, pray for the peace of departed souls and they also come here to die. After the great war of the Mahabharata at Kurukshetra, the Pandava brothers came to Kashi to perform the ritual of *prayaschitta* and atone for the sin of killing their family and friends. So did Lord Rama for the slaying of Ravana who was a brahmin. Lord Buddha walked through its labyrinth of lanes on his solitary path to Sarnath. The philosopher Adi Shankaracharya visited the hermitages to meet and debate with scholars. Nanak must have sat on these ghats with his companion Mardana to watch the sunrise over the river. Here Kabir and Tulsidas preached and sang as the temple bells rang at dawn and dusk. The Jain saint, the 23rd tirthankara Lord Parshvanath was born here.

They say that Varanasi is the oldest living city in the world. Once ancient cities like Babylon, Nineveh, and Luxor were its contemporaries. Today their temples lie silent and their city walls have vanished into the sand but Varanasi's lanes are still alive with people. Its temples echo to bells and *mantras* and its ghats teem with pilgrims. May be only Jerusalem can compare with its venerable sanctity. As M A Sherring wrote in reluctant admiration, "In any case, Benaras is a city of no mean antiquity. Twenty five centuries ago, at the least, it was famous. When Babylon was struggling with Nineveh for supremacy, when Tyre was planting her colonies, when Athens was growing in strength, before Rome had become known, or Greece contended with Persia... she had already risen to greatness, if not glory."

So it is a city that has seen everything and survived much. The armies of Mahmud of Ghazni, Alauddin Khalji and Aurangzeb have swept in to plunder the treasures of its temples and then demolished the shrines. For centuries Varanasi has lived with these hills of rubble as a reminder of its tragedy. No other *tirtha* has faced such ravages and still after every invasion the city has raised its head and built again. However for all its gallant courage, Kashi has paid a heavy price for being so beloved of its people. In spite of being the oldest living city in the world it has no temple that is more than three centuries old. The memories of great shrines like Vishweshwara, Avimukteshwara, Omkareshwar and Bindu Madhav are merely legends of a city that refuses to forget them. But Kashi, the great survivor, stands on hallowed ground where Shiva dances a happy tandava and the pilgrims have never stopped coming here.

Wandering along the dim, serpentine lanes of Varanasi is like taking a stroll all across this many hued land of India. It is a microcosm of the country and the air is filled with voices speaking in myriad languages. On a stroll along the Vishwanath Gali you may encounter Tamilian men with stripes of sandalwood paste across their foreheads and their docile wives in silks walking behind them. Voluble Bengalis arguing with shopkeepers in their loud and atrocious Hindi. Gujarati village women in huge skirts, their faces hidden behind bright veils and just a pair of wide kohled eyes turning to look at you.

On the busy steps of the Dasashwamedha Ghat you could meet a businessman from Bihar, a weaver from Andhra Pradesh or a matted haired sadhu in saffron from nowhere. And among them, wandering bemused and fascinated, the young men and women from the West wrapped in *namavalis* and jangling with *rudraksha* beads, looking for some mysterious, pagan salvation, exotic eastern experiences or just a *chillum* of bhang. Wise and cynical Kashi will give each of them what they are looking for because this city that seems older than time has seen so many like them before.

Varanasi does not believe in charming its visitors, it refuses to welcome with holiness and at times seems to take a perverse pleasure in being easy to dislike. As you see it first, it is just a very old city—decadent, dirty and noisy, with dilapidated buildings, cows, beggars at every corner and chaotic streets that are an assault on the senses. People come here seeking calm and contemplation or an answer to the pain of grief, and are ambushed at the temples and ghats by priests with ruthless, avaricious eyes. Like all *tirthas*, here religion is also very good business and no city knows it better then the cynical old Kashi. Some of those priestly families have lived off the hopes and pain of people for generations.

A pilgrim has to move beyond these surface disturbances to find the peace they are seeking. So be patient and Kashi will show you its serene, utterly beautiful face. And you find it most often by the banks of the Ganga, watching her ever flowing waters head inexorably towards the sea. Among the eighty *ghats* there are many that are deserted and one can sit there forever watching the sunrise turn the river to a liquid gold, touching the top of the waves with a bronze shimmer like the silk they weave here. As a boat with a tattered sail drifts by, somewhere behind you young voices are raised reciting Sanskrit *shlokas* in that familiar droning rhythm. Slowly the mind becomes quiet and every sorrow seems to recede. The magic of Kashi comes in such unexpected moments of serendipitous peace.

Surprisingly you can find this peace even in a crowded noisy temple. Standing there watching an aarti at the door of the *garbha griha*, as the priest raises the many flamed lamp to illumine the serene face of a goddess, the air echoing to the chant of *mantras*. Listen and you'll hear the woman standing beside you softly sing along. Here a rickshawalla wearing a torn vest will tell you an amusing myth about Shiva. A *paan* chewing foodshop owner will offer you a taste of his freshly made sweet *rabri* from his *karhai* of boiling milk. An ash smeared sadhu will speak to you in English and then laugh at your astonishment. You don't even have to be a believer for Kashi to seduce you with its unique, vibrant, contrary moods.

Do not go to Kashi with any expectations or pre-conceived notions and the city will surprise you with its humour, compassion and kindness. You only have to keep the windows of your mind open and eternal Kashi-Varanasi will speak to you. For centuries this *tirtha* has been loved by the faithful. It has that inexplicable power to bind the people of this diverse and often divided land with the ties of tradition and worship. When you come to Kashi, you have to seek that 'Light' within you that the Adi Shankaracharya is talking about. You can discover yourself in eternal Kashi.

Two

OM NAMAH SHIVAYA!

"Bending low in adoration, go round
The rock bearing the foot-print of the moon crested Lord.
Perpetually worshipped with offerings by siddhas;
Looking upon it, the body abandoned
And sins shaken off, the faithful gain
The Eternal Station of the Lord's attendants.

—Kalidasa, in praise of Shiva, *'Meghadutam'*
(trans. by Chandra Rajan)

Parvati, the loved and pampered daughter of Himalaya, the Lord of the Mountains, and his wife Mena had chosen a very strange bridegroom. He was an ascetic who lived on a mountain, wearing animal skins, his body smeared with ash and his matted hair tied in a topknot. The only jewellery he wore was brown *rudraksha* beads and instead of the shining armour of the other gods he carried a trident and a begging bowl. No parent would have chosen Shiva as a groom for his daughter and Himalaya was naturally not pleased with Parvati.

So on his wedding day Shiva decided to dress for the occasion. He was now clad in golden silk and instead of the snakes writhing around his neck, he wore flower garlands and strings of *bilva* leaves as necklaces. Instead of ash, his body was perfumed by sandalwood paste and he placed the silver crescent of the moon on his hair. The marriage was performed peacefully but Shiva's problems were not over. After this magnificent celestial marriage he could hardly take his new bride to live in a cave on Mount Kailash. So Parvati and Shiva began to search the earth for a place to stay. Going along the river Ganga they saw the golden spires of palaces, tall gateways and verdant gardens of a city and Shiva immediately fell in love with the place and came to stay there. This city that enchanted this moody, mendicant god was Kashi-Varanasi.

Kashi is said to stand on the trident of Shiva. The city is spread over three low hills that stand beside the Ganga and these hills are believed to be the three prongs of the trident. The *Kashi Khanda* describes the city as having streets studded with jewels, palaces with golden *shikharas* soaring to the sky and decorated by flying banners. Shiva so loved his earthly home that he vowed never to forsake it. This is why Varanasi is Avimukta, never forsaken by Shiva and all the gods and goddesses who reside here. Shiva and Parvati turned the city into a garden of happiness and so it is their Anandavana. One of the ancient names of the city is Rudravasa, the city of Rudra-Shiva and many old *shlokas* call it by that name. Finally it is also Mahashmashana because Shiva who wanders in cremation grounds is also the god who offers *nirvana* to the souls of his devotees. For the true devotee of course Banaras is everywhere. As Devara Dasimayya, the Seventh century Tamil poet wrote,

> "To the utterly at one with Siva
> There's no dawn, no new moon
> No noonday, nor equinoxes
> Nor sunsets, nor full moons
> His front yard is the true Benaras
> O Ramanatha!"

The presence of Shiva permeates the atmosphere of Varanasi. They say, "Kashi ka har kankar boley Shiva Shankar", that every pebble of Kashi sings of Shiva. There are *shivalingams* everywhere—under trees, in tiny shrines tucked into a niche in the wall, in the corners of houses and beside the steps of the ghats. Every home has a shrine to Shiva lit by brass lamps and perfumed by incense sticks and every shop will have his picture on the wall. His image is painted on the doorway of houses, printed on calendars and sketched on the sides of the boats. For the people he is their beloved Baba, a benign presence that is a part of their lives. As they come out of the river after their morning baths they carry a pot full of Ganga water to pour over a nearby lingam praying to Shiva. They exclaim by intoning "Shiva! Shiva!" The seasons are marked by his *pujas* and festivals and they all hope to die in the city so that kind old Baba will be there to hold their hand through the great crossing.

Shiva is Ishvara, the great god and like Vishnu his worship reverberates across the land. As the third member of the divine trinity with Brahma, the creator, and Vishnu, the preserver, he has the terrible role of the destroyer. Once the creation of Brahma has run its course and reached the final stage of the last age of Kali Yuga, Shiva destroys it all, so that the cycle of creation can begin once again. He dances the maddened cosmic dance of the *tandava* and everything is destroyed under his dancing feet and then his third eye opens and its fierce rays burn it all to ashes.

The sect that worships Shiva are called Shaivas and the temples dedicated to the god can be found in every city and village in the land. The worship of Shiva is founded on surrender and asceticism and less on the tender devotion practised by the devotees of Vishnu, the Vaishnavas. It appeals to the questioning and meditative mind and the Shaiva faith attracts people as it is less bound by the rules of caste or religious ritual. Shiva is a tolerant god and some of the greatest mystic poets who wrote hymns to Shiva belonged to the lower castes.

Shiva's devotees have ranged from kings to potters, weavers and hunters and among them the most famous are the Nayanmar poets of the south. Poets like Basavanna, Sambandar, Appar and Sundarar sang to the many moods of this unconventional god, trying to capture his quicksilver character as they surrendered to the worship of Shiva. Like true lovers they all gave him their own names. Basavanna called him 'Lord of the meeting rivers'. For the poetess Mahadeviakka he was "my lord white as jasmines" and Allama Prabhu called him "Lord of the caves". As Sambandar wrote in the seventh century,

> "The serpent is his ear stud, he rides a bull
> He is crowned with the pure white crescent
> He is smeared with the ashes of destroyed forests
> He is decked with a garland of full blossoming flowers
> When his devotees call him he comes glittering
> And bestows his grace upon all.
> He is indeed the thief who has stolen my soul away."

Shiva intrigues both the believer and the scholar because he is such a contrary god, with both ascetic and ecstatic tendencies. He is the ambiguous lord of darkness and light, death and creation, a complex blend of compassion and quick anger, generosity and impatience. He is the enigmatic god of ascetics but is also a family man married to Parvati. He can wander about wearing animal skins in the company of ghosts and goblins and he also enjoys adorning himself in silks and flowers. He is indifferent to pleasure but the lingam is also a symbol of creation and regeneration. He is the outcaste among gods and the champion of the outsider but kings have worshipped and built temples dedicated to him. He is often in a state of genial intoxication and can generate a mystic fervour in his devotees. He is capable of a mystical stillness and of the kinetic movement of dance. Like a chameleon, Shiva encompasses every human feeling and experience and that is why he is so beloved of his devotees.

Unlike the majestic Vishnu resplendent in silks and jewels, Shiva is usually depicted as a wandering mendicant, wrapped in a tiger skin, with his bare body smeared with the ash from cremation grounds. His matted locks are piled on top of his head in a knot, within his locks hides the river goddess Ganga and the crescent moon glows above his forehead. He wears a necklace of *rudraksha* beads and uses *rudrakshas* for his meditation. He carries a small rattle drum, the Damaru; a trident, the Trishula and a begging bowl. The Trishula is his favourite weapon but he is also the divine archer and uses a giant bow called Pinaka.

Across his forehead are drawn the three stripes called the *tripundraka* and in the centre is the third eye that is a symbol of wisdom and also his anger. Snakes writhe around his neck like a living necklace and beside him sits his vehicle, the Nandi bull. Unlike other gods he has no celestial palace in heaven. He lives in a cave on Mount Kailash in the Himalayas and on earth he lives in Varanasi.

Shiva is not an ancient Aryan god like Indra or Varuna. Vishnu was at least mentioned in the Vedas, Shiva does not appear at all in Vedic literature. His beginnings are traced to an obscure Vedic god called Rudra who got just two and a half hymns dedicated to him in the *Rig Veda*. One of the hymns praising Rudra says,

> "Tawny boar of the sky, dreaded form with braided hair.
> We call you down and we bow low.

Holding in his hand the healing medicines that we long for,
Let him grant us protection, shelter, refuge."

Shiva does share many of the characteristics of Rudra but the god who rose to eminence in the epic period was a much more complex deity who had evolved from many local gods and their cults. The people of the Indus Valley Civilization had a god of the animals that scholars call Pashupati, who resembles Shiva. As depicted on the Harappan seals, it is a figure sitting in a yogic posture, wearing a horned headdress and surrounded by animals. This god was also worshipped in his phallic symbol of the lingam and this phallic worship continues to be an important part of the cult of Shiva.

As Varanasi is called Rudravasa, 'the home of Rudra', one of Shiva's many names is Rudra, the "angry one" and the "yeller." This minor god of the Vedas possesses few gentle qualities. He is merely a manifestation of Agni, the god of fire, and the Maruts, the gods of the storms, are his sons. In other hymns he is treated as a separate deity who is the lord of sacrifices and a healing god of animals. However he is also an angry god who often shouts out in rage and the hymns are songs trying to calm his anger. He is described as having a red skin, a blue neck and a thousand eyes. He rides a chariot carrying a thunderbolt, bows and arrows and is "as terrible as a wild beast, destructive and fierce". At another place he is described as "dark, black, destroying, terrible". And one hymn intriguingly calls him "the bountiful, the lord of spirits and the lord of thieves". As the Svetasvatara Upanishad declares,

"There is one, Rudra alone.
Who rules the world in his might.
He stands behind all beings
He made all the worlds and protects them
And rolls them up at the end of time."

Shiva appears as a complete god with his own myths in the two great Indian epics—the *Ramayana* and the *Mahabharata*. In the *Ramayana*, Lord Rama breaks the bow that Shiva had given to King Janaka and wins Sita as his bride. Later when Rama is preparing to cross the sea to invade Lanka, this *avatar* of Vishnu worships Shiva at Rameshwaram. Ravana, the king of Lanka was also a great devotee of Shiva and there are myths about how Ravana had performed severe austerities to gain Shiva's blessings and boons.

The Mahabharata has passages that call Vishnu supreme and others that praise Shiva as Mahadeva, the great god. It must have been a time of strife between the devotees of the two deities because the epic is full of mutual claims of superiority. Also there are more conciliatory passages by writers saying that in the final analysis Shiva and Vishnu are the same. One passage in the *Harivamsa*, trying to reconcile the two warring sects, says there is "no difference between Shiva who exists in the form of Vishnu and Vishnu who exists in the form of Shiva". In Varanasi the myths around the *ghats* of Manikarnika and Adi Keshava weave in tales of Vishnu and Shiva.

Shiva is Mahadeva, the greatest of the gods and the *Matsya, Kurma, Linga, Shiva, Skanda* and *Agni puranas* were all written in praise of Shiva and many of his myths are found in them. In many myths there is a conflict between Shiva and the other gods and he comes out triumphant or Brahma and Vishnu are shown seeking his help. During the great churning of the ocean when the poison flowing out of the mouth of the snake Vasuki was about to ruin the earth, Vishnu prayed to Shiva to come and rescue Prithvi, the goddess earth. Shiva drank the poison and it turned his throat blue leading to his name Neelkantha, the blue-throated. There are myths around the temples of Varanasi that have Brahma building a shrine to Shiva at Brahmeshwar on Dasashwamedha Ghat and of Vishnu praying to Shiva at the Adi Keshava Temple.

It is natural for such a volatile and paradoxical god that the name Shiva means 'auspicious' and 'gentle'. He is Mahakala, the great destroyer and the great time and Nataraja, the Lord of the Cosmic Dance who inspired the text of classical dance, the *Natya Shastra*. However, in Hindu belief, destruction and creation are in the same cycle, so Shiva or Shankara is also auspicious as he begins the new cycle of creation. For the Shaiva, his god Shiv-Shankara is creator, preserver and destroyer. The *Shivalingam* is the symbol of this creative force of Shiva and this phallic symbol is worshipped more often than his images. Most of the Shiva temples in Varanasi worship a *Shivalingam* and the most sacred are the *jyotirlingams* of Omkareshwar, Vishweshwar, Avimukteshwar and Kedareshwar.

The Myth of the Jyotirlingam

The *jyotirlingam* myth tells the story of the appearance of the first lingam on earth. *Jyotirlingam* means the *lingam* of the effulgent light. The story begins with the trinity of Brahma,

Vishnu and Shiva not being able to agree as to who was the greatest among them. So they consulted the four Vedas, the source of all knowledge and the Vedas said that Shiva was supreme. Both Brahma and Vishnu were naturally reluctant to accept this verdict, at which volatile Shiva lost his temper and transformed himself into an endless column of glittering light that pierced the sky, the earth and the netherworld. In Varanasi they say that the site of the city marks the spot where the *jyotirlingam* appeared on earth.

Brahma and Vishnu were curious about where this fiery column began and where it ended. Vishnu turned himself into a boar and began to dig deep into the earth while Brahma flew up to the sky on the back of his swan. They travelled for thousands of years but still could not discover the two ends of the column. When they returned to earth, Vishnu was honest enough to admit that he had failed in his quest. At this the column of light became smaller and turned into a *Shivalingam* and Vishnu thus worshipped Shiva.

Brahma however was in no mood to admit his defeat. He claimed that he had seen the end of the column in the sky and he even called a *ketaki* flower to bear false witness and support his claim. Shiva, not the most patient of the gods, finally lost his temper and turned into a raging Bhairava and cut off one of Brahma's five heads. That is why Brahma now has only four heads.

However, Shiva's problems were not over yet. Brahma was also the first brahmin of the world and there is no greater sin than killing a brahmin. To Shiva's horror the skull of Brahma's severed head stuck to his hand and would not come off. Shiva performed many penances and performed long pilgrimages to all the important *tirthasthanas* but could not free himself from it. Finally he arrived in Varanasi where his penances were successful and the skull fell off. The temple of Kapalamochan, meaning 'where the head fell' marks that spot. This is another reason why Varanasi is Shiva's favourite city.

Created from pure light, the *jyotirlingams* are also called Swayambhu, 'self created'. There are twelve *jyotirlingams* in the country and the most sacred ones are at Kedarnath, Rameshwaram and in Varanasi. Here three temples claim to have the *jyotirlingam*—the old Omkareshwar temple, which is today a forgotten temple near Trilochana Ghat. Then there is the main Kashi Vishwanath temple with the two *lingams* of Vishweshwar and Avimukteshwar and the *lingam* at the ancient Kedareshwar temple that stands on top of the Kedar Ghat.

Brahma after losing his fifth head became Chaturanana while Shiva is at times depicted with five heads as Panchanana. His five faces illustrate his five cosmic functions of creation, conservation, destruction, incarnation and liberation. Each face has a different expression and together they capture both his accessible and obscure nature. First there is Shrishti, the face of creation and then Sthiti, the face of preservation. The terrible face of destruction is called Samhara, usually depicted with an angry open mouth. The fourth is of Shiva who is hard to comprehend as he is concealed as Tirobhava. Finally there is the utterly calm and indescribable fifth face of compassion, revelation and salvation called Anugraha.

As Shiva is the Mahayogi, the great ascetic, he lives the life of a nomadic mendicant, wandering in cremation grounds covered in ash, wearing a garland of skulls, accompanied by ghosts and goblins. His devotees often practise the system of meditation called yoga. There is also the Tantric way of worshipping him. That is an obscure, rather esoteric cult. It also worships the goddess as Shakti using complex spells, sacred formulas and secret rituals known only to the initiates. The form of Buddhism popular in Tibet has absorbed some of these Tantric practices involving Shiva and the goddess Shakti. Some other Shaiva sects are the Lingayat, Vira Shaiva, Pasupata, Lakulisa and Kapalika.

Shiva is Digambara, the naked or sky clad, and Dhurjati, with matted hair. This lord of the paradox likes to consume intoxicating drugs and drinks and then he dances as snakes writhe around his blue throat. But this terrible face does not repulse his devotees, to whom he still looks hypnotically handsome. This aspect of Shiva appeals to the dark, fearful side of the human mind, where nightmares lurk. The Indian sadhu or sannyasin with their tridents and begging bowls are the living images of the Mahayogi.

Shiva's rather unique garments have also gathered their own myths. Once when the great *yogi* was wandering in the forest he came upon the *ashrams* of *rishis* and here the wives of the *rishis* fell in love with the handsome ascetic. Angered by this, the *rishis* conjured up a tiger to attack him but when the tiger sprang, Shiva killed it with the nail of his little finger, stripped off its skin and wore it around his body. The *rishis* sent serpents and he wrapped them around his throat like garlands. Finally a demon dwarf, Apasmara, was unleashed on him and Shiva danced on it and it stayed forever under his foot. Finally the *rishis* realised who this young *yogi* was and worshipped him.

Daksha's Sacrifice

Many of the myths portray Shiva as an outsider in the assembly of gods and this reflects the time when the worship of the non-Vedic Shiva was still being resisted by the Aryan Brahmin priesthood. Shiva and the Devi were deities of the people whose popularity forced the priesthood to admit them into the Hindu pantheon. Even today Shiva's simple rituals of worship and symbols reflect his non-Vedic, Dravidian beginnings. Among all the myths the one around the sacrifice of Daksha illustrates this stage of transition the most clearly, as the Vedic gods are first forced to admit his superiority and then are eclipsed by the power of Shiva.

The story of Daksha's great sacrifice first appears in the *Brahmanas*. Daksha was a son of Brahma and as a Prajapati, he was one of the fathers of the human race. Among his many daughters was the beautiful Sati who chose to marry Shiva. This did not please Daksha as Shiva was hardly an ideal groom. The Vedic gods lived like kings in celestial palaces, travelled in chariots, wore silks and jewels. While Shiva could only offer a mountain home to his bride and the life of a wandering ascetic. However as Sati was adamant and even Brahma wanted the marriage to take place, Daksha allowed her to marry Shiva.

Daksha was angered even more when at a gathering of the gods all the others got up to greet him except Brahma and Shiva, who both remained seated. Brahma, as his father, was rightfully waiting to be greeted by him. But Shiva's action was taken as a deliberate insult by Daksha. So when Daksha decided to hold a big sacrifice he invited every god in heaven except Shiva. Sati saw the chariots of the gods all heading for the sacrifice and in spite of Shiva asking her not to, she insisted on going to her father's home.

At the assembly of gods Daksha explained his not inviting Shiva in these words that capture beautifully Shiva's paradoxical and socially outcast nature, "What is his lineage and what is his clan? What place does he belong to and what is his nature? What does he do for a living and how does he behave? This fellow who drinks poison and rides a bull. He is not an ascetic, for how can one who carries a weapon be an ascetic? He is not a householder for he lives in the cremation ground. He is not a celibate student, for he has a wife. And he cannot be a forest dweller, for he is drunk with the conceit of his lordship. He is not a Brahmin, for the *Vedas* do not know him as one." And so it goes on, describing an interloper into the pantheon of the Vedic gods.

On the day of the sacrifice when Sati arrived, she was insulted by her father and deeply hurt she jumped into the *yajna* fire and died. Hearing of her death an enraged Shiva appeared at the gathering with his matted locks flaring around his head like flames. Two demons appeared from these locks named Virbhadra and Bhadrakali and they destroyed the sacrifice and then attacked the gods. No god could face their rage as they cut off Daksha's head, knocked off Pushan's teeth, Bhrigu lost all his hair and they plucked out Bhaga's eyes. As chaos reigned Vishnu finally had to intervene and he persuaded the gods to worship Shiva.

As his anger cooled Shiva called back his demons and allowed the sacrifice to continue. Daksha was brought back to life but with the head of a goat. Later Sati would be reborn as Parvati, the beautiful daughter of the Himalayas and his wife Mena. Shiva, reluctant to marry again, was by then absorbed in meditation and Parvati would perform many penances to finally win his hand. After marrying Parvati, Shiva would look for a home on earth and choose the city of Varanasi.

Shiva and King Divodasa of Varanasi

The most interesting myth of Shiva and Varanasi is about how once the god was forced to leave his beloved city. It all began when the earth was cursed by a terrible drought that lasted for sixty years and Brahma feared that his creation would be destroyed. He needed a king of such perfect virtue that his presence would once again restore the blessings of nature on earth. There was only one such man, King Ripunjaya who had taken *sanyas* and was living as a *rishi* in Varanasi.

Ripunjaya was willing to become king of the world but on one condition. He was going to rule from Varanasi and he did not want any interference from the gods. So all the gods who lived in Varanasi had to return to their homes in heaven. All the other gods readily agreed but Shiva was very reluctant to leave. However finally he agreed to go and live on Mount Mandara as the mountain was a devotee and had been praying for a long time that Shiva should come and live there. Finally Varanasi had no gods and Ripunjaya ascended the throne, taking the ironic title of Divodasa, 'servant of the gods'.

King Divodasa was a truly righteous king and his reign saw the earth recover and become prosperous again. The people were happy, peace and justice prevailed. But living on

Mount Mandara, Shiva was pining for his beloved Varanasi. He decided that the only way Divodasa could fall from grace was to make him commit a moral or ethical mistake. His power would wane if he failed in his *dharma* and then the gods could return to Kashi. And for that Shiva had to tempt him in some way.

First sixty-four female demi-goddesses called *yoginis* were sent to Kashi by Shiva, with instructions to use their wiles to corrupt the king. The *yoginis* entered the city in various disguises as dancers, garland makers and fortune tellers and for a year tried to create trouble but they could not tempt Divodasa. Instead, they were themselves changed by the atmosphere of *dharma* in Kashi. They gave up their seductive ways and decided to stay on in the city as its citizens. These sixty four *yoginis* are still worshipped in the Chaunsathi Devi temple in the city.

Shiva next turned to the sun god Surya for help. Surya also wandered the city in many disguises seeking some immorality in the city but could find none. Then like the *yoginis* he too chose to stay forever in this city of *dharma*. Surya decided to divide himself into twelve Adityas and spread his golden rays across the city. One of the twelve adityas is Lolarka, the 'trembling sun' and there is a famous pool called the Lolarka Kund near Asi Ghat where a popular festival is held every rainy season.

A disappointed Shiva now begged Brahma to help him return to his city. Brahma disguised himself as a brahmin priest and went to the court of Divodasa. He requested that the king help him in performing ten *ashvamedha* sacrifices, this being the most intricate of sacrifices needing elaborate preparations and with very complicated rituals. Brahma hoped that Divodasa would make a mistake somewhere but the sacrifices were performed with flawless *dharma*. The site of these sacrifices is the Dasashwamedha ghat, the holiest ghat in Kashi. Bathing here still brings the blessings of those ten sacrifices of Divodasa. Then like all the others before him, Brahma too decided to stay in Varanasi.

In this way all the gods were gradually returning in secret to Kashi but poor Shiva was still sitting heartbroken on Mt. Mandara. Now he turned to the cleverest of the gods, his son Lord Ganesha. When he arrived in Kashi, Ganesha took the guise of a brahmin fortune teller and one of the queens of Divodasa told the king of this man who could see into the future. Divodasa invited Ganesha into his palace and confessed that after so many years of ruling the world he was a tired man and was seeking peace and liberation. Ganesha predicted that in eighteen days a wise brahmin would arrive in Kashi and he would have the answer to all Divodasa's dilemmas. Then Ganesha waited for the arrival of Lord Vishnu in Kashi.

Lord Vishnu arrived in Kashi and first bathed at the confluence of the Varuna and Ganga rivers at a place called Paduka Tirtha, where the Adi Keshava ghat now stands. The Adi Keshava temple is the oldest shrine to Vishnu in the city. Vishnu transformed himself into a Buddhist monk named Punyakriti and his consort, the goddess Sri became a Buddhist nun named Vijnanakaumudi. They now began to teach the Buddhist message that went against the *dharma* of caste and denied the existence of a supreme creator. As people followed their teachings and denied caste and religion, society began to break down and chaos took over.

Divodasa watched helplessly as his kingdom of perfect *dharma* began to disintegrate. Now he waited anxiously for the eighteenth day when the wise brahmin would arrive. When Vishnu entered Divodasa's court the old king admitted his fatigue and need for peace and *nirvana*. Vishnu said Divodasa's mistake was in expelling Shiva from Kashi and the solution lay in the presence of Shiva in the city. So Divodasa should establish a *lingam* in Kashi and then the gods will take him to heaven.

So Divodasa placed his son on the throne, established a *lingam* called Divodaseshwara, near Mir ghat, that he worshipped and then a celestial chariot took him to heaven. In Kashi all the *yoginis*, Surya, Brahma, Ganesha and Vishnu who had refused to leave the beautiful city now waited for the arrival of Shiva. In preparation for Shiva's arrival, Vishnu bathed again at the pool of five rivers called Panchanada, where the Panchganga ghat now stands.

A triumphant Shiva entered Kashi in a celestial chariot made by elements of the entire cosmos. The Ganga and the Yamuna rivers were the shafts of the chariot. The gods of the morning and evening were the two wheels and Vayu the wind god moved the wheels. Akash, the sky was the umbrella over his head, the sun and the moon guarded the doors and Mount Meru was the flagpole. The stars and the heavens were the nails that held the chariot together. Dakshina, the ritual gift to one's guru became the axle, Pranava, the mystical syllable became the seat and Gayatri, the Vedic chant became the footrest. All the gods welcomed Shiva and Parvati with a ceremonious *aarti* at a place called Vrishabhadhvaja, where they first saw Shiva's flag with the bull emblem. Shiva and Parvati were finally home in their beloved Varanasi-Kashi.

Like all myths, the story of Divodasa also contains a kernel of history. It talks of the time when Buddhism was ascendant in the land and Brahminical Hinduism was in retreat in Kashi. Sarnath with its monasteries had become the main place of pilgrimage and pilgrims came less to Kashi, thus depriving the gods and brahmins of their offerings. Then there was a revival of Hinduism and Kashi returned to its position as the pre-eminent *tirtha*. The myth also explains how in spite of being Shiva's special place, Varanasi also contains the temples of all the gods, goddesses and demi-deities like *yoginis* and *yakshas*.

Among the temples to other deities, some of the most important ones are dedicated to the various aspects of Devi, the Mother Goddess. She is worshipped as Annapurna, Durga and Vishalakshi. Shiva is always linked with Shakti—the female power of Devi. So the mendicant Shiva is also portrayed as a family man with wife Parvati and children. And like her consort, the Devi is also a goddess with many faces. She can be the generous food bearing Annapurna and the fierce warrior goddess Durga or the death-maddened Kali.

Shiva and Parvati's two sons are Kartikeya, who is the commander-in-chief of the army of the gods and Ganesha, the benign elephant-headed god of good fortune. When Shiva is the Mahayogi and the wanderlust hits him he wanders among the ghosts and goblins in places connected with death like cremation grounds, battlefields and crossroads. He is accompanied by his two companions Nandi and Bhringi. Nandi is also the bull that is Shiva's chosen vehicle.

Merciful Shiva is also very generous with his boons. Even demons like Hiranyakasipu and Ravana have performed difficult austerities and earned boons from him that have put the gods in danger. He gave the Pasupata weapon to Arjuna and the battleaxe to Parashuram. Yudhishthira received a weapon called Shakta, King Janaka got a bow and Rama received powerful arrows.

There are great temples dedicated to Shiva all across the land. The Pallava kings built temples dedicated to him at their capital Kanchipuram, including the magnificent Kailasanatha Temple. The Chola king Raja Raja built the gigantic Brihadeeshwara temple in Thanjavur. Shiva's most sacred temple in the Himalayas is at Kedarnath and devotees also worship the remote Kailash Mountain. The temple at Rameshwaram is sacred because Lord Rama worshipped Shiva here with a lingam made with sand by Sita. The Elephanta caves have some of the greatest sculptures of Shiva including the majestic three headed Mahadeva image.

The icons of Shiva show him in a multitude of moods. The most famous and also the most visually pleasing depiction is as Nataraja, the lord of the dance and lord of the actors. He dances the *tandava* that Ananda Coomaraswamy calls "the manifestation of primal energy". Shiva stands with one foot raised in a fluid movement of dancing, his hair flowing out like a halo around his head. One hand holds the *damaru* drum, the other a deer, the third a ball of fire and the fourth points to his foot that rests on Apasmara, the dwarf of ignorance. The figure is circled by an aureole of flames.

As Kalyanasundara Murti Shiva is the handsome young ascetic the women fall in love with and as the mystic poet Mahadeviakka sings,

> My husband comes home today
> Wear your best, wear your jewels
> The Lord, white as jasmine,
> Will come anytime now,
> Girls, come, meet Him at the door.

As Tripurantaka he is the divine archer who used the Pinaka bow to destroy three demon cities with just one arrow. As Hari-Hara, half his body is of Shiva and the other of Vishnu. While as the androgynous Ardhanarishwara, the other half is the female Shakti. As Somaskanda he sits with Parvati, both dressed like royalty with their son Kartikeya in the middle. Shiva's image is shown within a lingam as Shiva Lingodbhava and his five faces of shrishti, sthiti, samhara, tirobhava and anugraha form a lingam in Mukhalinga.

As Yogeshwara he is a handsome young ascetic and when this ascetic is depicted as begging for alms he is Bhikshayatana. As Pinaki and Kirata he carries bows and arrows and is the greatest archer of the pantheon. In one of his most attractive aspects Shiva is Gyana Dakshinamurti, the handsome young teacher, sitting under a tree facing the south, with one leg crossed at the knee, his wild hair framing a calm compassionate face, with his right hand raised in the posture of teaching.

Shiva's greatest festival is Shivaratri, the 'night of Shiva', when he is worshipped with nightlong prayers and all Varanasi sways in celebration. On this moonless *amavasya* night in spring, in the month of Phalguna, Shiva is said to have married Parvati. It is also said that he dances the tandava on Shivaratri. In Varanasi the biggest celebration is held at the Kashi Vishwanath temple with all night prayers and singing of hymns, with people crowding the narrow lanes throughout the day and night. Then at midnight a resplendent Lord Shiva is taken out on a celebratory chariot ride across his beloved city.

Shiva has one thousand and one names. The hundred names of Rudra called Shatarudriya is often recited by his devotees like a *mantra*. He is Shankara, tranquil and auspicious; Gangadhara, the bearer of the Ganga; Chandrashekhara, the moon crested and Girisha, the lord of the mountains. He is Mrityunjaya, one who has defeated death; Mahakala, the great time; Ishana, the celestial ruler; Kedara, who lives in the mountains and Pashupati, the lord of animals.

Shiva is also Shambhu, the auspicious; Mahesha, the great lord and Vishwanatha, the lord of the world. As Tryambaka he is three eyed; Hara is the seizer and Aghora, the terrible. The Mahayogi is also Bhuteshwar, the lord of ghosts; Vyomkesa has hair like the sky and Ashutosh is a god who is easily pleased. Shiva is also Rudra, the yeller, Nilalohit, the blue red god, Ghorani, the terrible and Diptani, the shining. In Varanasi of course he is first and always Kashinath and Kashipati, the resplendent and beloved lord of Kashi.

Three

UNFORGETTABLE GANGA
River of Life and Liberation

"Gange cha Yamune chaiva Godavari, Saraswati.
Narmade, Sindhu, Kaveri, jale asmin sannidhin kuru"
—Sanskrit shloka praising the seven holy rivers.

Since ancient times Hindus have said this prayer in praise of the seven most sacred rivers of the land as they took their morning dip in a river or a pond. Wherever they may be, in a village or a city, in the hills or by the sea they have beseeched these rivers to purify and liberate them by their holy waters. In this shloka, singing the praises of Ganga, Yamuna, Godavari, Saraswati, Narmada, Sindhu (Indus) and Kaveri, the one river that is named first, even before the mighty Indus is the Ganga.

The Ganga, divine and earthly, a mighty river whose waters purify, Mother Goddess, both giver of life and liberation after death. Serene and gently flowing or tempestuous and destructively angry, it is a river that is woven into the fabric of our land. Often present in its symbolism, religion, rituals, history and mythology, folk tales, songs and dances. As it flows across the plains of north India this majestic river is a legend like the Nile or the Amazon and for Hindus its flowing waters encapsulate the magic and mystery of life itself.

There are many rivers in the world which are broader and longer than the Ganga. In the Indian subcontinent itself there are the Indus and the Brahmaputra but none of them possess the many hued character of this river. It is so much more than just a river to the people who live beside her and the millions who come to the holy cities rising by her banks to take a ritual dip in its sanctified waters. The Ganga is a part of their primeval memory, their heritage and their hope of salvation.

This wise, compassionate, old river has seen so much. It has seen kingdoms rise and fall by its banks, the avarice of conquerors and the simplicity of the pilgrim. It has watched preachers and poets sit by its flowing waters and inspired their words and fired their imagination. It has watered fields, making them fertile with her generous silt and relentlessly swept away villages in angry floods. Somewhere it possesses that inexplicable, mythical quality that makes it not just another grand river but a truly great one.

This is not merely a river, it is India itself. As Lord Krishna says in the *Bhagavat Gita,*

"Among the purifiers, I am the wind.
I am Rama among the warriors.
I am the shark among the fish.
I am the Ganga among the rivers."

The Ganga begins its journey high in the remote, snowy ranges of the Garhwal Himalayas. They call this region—Devabhoomi—the land of the gods. It is a visually majestic landscape of pine forests, steep mountain tracks and rushing hill streams through which pilgrims and ascetics have travelled for centuries to the temple of Gangotri that is dedicated to the Goddess Ganga. After a twenty kilometre trek from the temple of Gangotri the pilgrim trail ends at Gaumukh, 4500 metres above sea level where the river actually emerges from the immense expanse of the Gangotri glacier. This glacier is a sea of ice nearly thirty kilometres long surrounded by snow-capped peaks ringed with clouds. Here, from an ice cave festooned with icicles called Gaumukh, the Cow's Mouth, the river emerges and as the ancient sages said, may be it really does emerge from Lord Shiva, the ascetic's tangled, top knotted head.

Emerging from Gaumukh, the river rushes past the little village of Gangotri. Here, just for a few kilometres, the river meanders north and that gives the place its name of the Ganga moving "uttara". Here the river is called Bhagirathi because it is said that King Bhagirath prayed to the river goddess here at Gangotri and persuaded the celestial stream to turn her path and come down to earth.

In the beginning the Ganga, a daughter of the Himalayas, was a goddess, a celestial river that flowed out of Vishnu's toe and then spread her silver waters in Swarga, the kingdom of the gods. It is her descent to earth that brought life and plenty to people. The myth of her coming to earth begins with King Sagara, of the Ikshvaku clan and an ancestor of Lord Rama, who had become so powerful that even the gods became envious. Then like all ambitious monarchs Sagara performed the *ashwamedha yajna*, which rivalled those performed by the gods. In this sacrifice a horse was sent off to wander the neighbouring kingdoms and wherever it went unchallenged became a part of the kingdom of the king.

Lord Indra, the king of the gods, could not bear the growing power of Sagara and stole the horse and hid it in the hermitage of the sage, Kapil Muni. Finding the horse missing Sagara sent out his sixty thousand sons to search for it. In their search they dug so deep they reached the centre of the earth and in this way the oceans were created. Then they discovered the horse in the hermitage and believing that Kapil Muni had taken it, the foolish princes insulted the sage. Angered at being disturbed at his meditations and then being accused of stealing a horse, Kapil Muni opened his eyes and the heat of his rage burnt the sons of Sagara into ashes.

The ashes of Sagara's sons lay by the sea and the king knew that the only way his cursed progeny could gain salvation was when the ashes were washed away by the sacred waters of the Ganga. He and later his descendants prayed to the river goddess but she was reluctant to come down to earth. Finally Sagara's great-grandson, King Bhagirath went up to the Himalayas and performed such severe austerities that a reluctant Ganga finally had to agree.

The river goddess turned the path of her waters towards the earth but in her anger she flowed with such power that Brahma feared that her tumultuous torrents would wash away all creation itself. In desperation he turned to Shiva for help and the great yogi obligingly placed his matted haired head in the path of the cascading river to break her fall. As she meandered through the "labyrinth of his matted hair, the river lost her force and descended gently on earth, bestowing life along her course".

So Bhagirath walked eastwards from the Himalayas and the river followed behind and their journey covered the plains of North India to the sea. The ashes of Sagara's sons were purified at Ganga Sagar, on the Bay of Bengal and they finally gained liberation. As Kalidasa tells his wandering cloud in his poem *Meghadutam* about where to seek the Ganga,

> "From there you should visit Jahnu's daughter
> Near Kanakhala's hill, where she comes down.
> The slopes of the Lord of Mountains, making
> A stairway for Sagara's sons going up to heaven.
> She grasped Shiva's matted hair
> Clinging with wave-hands to the crest jewel of the moon.
> Foam laughter mocking the frown on Gauri's face."

So Shiva wears two decorations in his hair—the Ganga and the moon that he had picked up during the churning of the sea of milk. He allowed Ganga to flow out of the coils of his hair as seven streams that flowed and merged along the path to finally become the mighty Ganga. These seven streams are Bhagirathi, Alakananda, Mandakini, Yamuna, Nandakini, Pindar Ganga and Dhauli Ganga and a pilgrimage of bathing in all their waters is called the Sapta Samudri Tirtha. These confluences, the spots where these rivers meet, are called Prayags and they are also places of pilgrimage. There are five prayags in the Garhwal Hills along the course of the river between Gangotri and Haridwar.

The mythological imagery of a river flowing through the tangled locks of Shiva captures beautifully the many streams flowing through the hills to merge and swell their waters. The Alakananda flows past the pilgrim town of Badrinath and various rivers flow into her along the way. At Vishnu Prayag the Dhauli Ganga meets the Alakananda and at Nanda Prayag the smaller Nandakini flows into its turbulent waters. As the river flows southwards, at Karna Prayag the Pindar Ganga merges into it and at Rudra Prayag the Mandakini flows into the Alakananda. Finally at Deva Prayag the Alakananda surging down from the east meets the mighty Bhagirathi coming from Gangotri and from here the river is called the Ganga. The seventh stream to flow into the Ganga is the Yamuna and that confluence takes place further downstream in the plains at the Triveni Sangam of Allahabad.

From Deva Prayag the Ganga is a majestic river, broad, deep, turbulent and at times an impressively scary sight. A huge tumultuous torrent of waters flowing down a deep gorge, crashing against boulders, frothing against the rocks on the side, flowing down rapids in an almighty roar. Looking down at its mercurial, swift travelling waters you understand why Shiva had to offer his unprotected head in her path, this primal force of nature could only destroy.

When the brown-green waters of the Ganga emerge from the Shivalik hills and enters the plains at Rishikesh it is beginning to become calmer. Now it begins to spread its expanse across the plains. By the time it reaches Haridwar the celestial river is earthbound and not a young, rebellious stream any more. Here they worship the river goddess with flaming oil lamps every evening during an elaborate and visually dramatic *arati*. As dusk falls, priests walk up to the river bank carrying huge brass lamps lit with a multitude of flames. Then to the beat of drums, cymbals and bells, the blowing of conchs, the echoing intoning of *mantras* and the wafting of incense, the river is worshipped with flowers and leaping flames. While pilgrims float leaf bowls with small lamps on the water making their beloved Ganga glitter like a bejewelled dancer.

After Haridwar, the river moves across the flat expanse of Uttar Pradesh. Many smaller rivers—Gomti, Sone, Gaghra, Gandak flow into her as if paying their respect to the goddess by merging into her welcoming waters. The landscape by its banks begins to change. Rocky hills fade away to flat fields of wheat and sugarcane. Villages of thatched huts and mango groves stand by its side and the village women come to bathe and wash their clothes, cattle wallow as little boys leap and dive into the water. Now the Ganga is a giver of life, kinder and more gentle. Though even here, during the monsoons it can turn into a fierce, mud brown torrent that covers the fields with silt and washes away the huts, people and cattle.

At Allahabad the Yamuna and the mysterious Saraswati create a triple confluence and the Triveni comes alive to the congregation of the Kumbh Mela every twelve years. Then the Ganga heads for Shiva's city, Varanasi where it is loved and worshipped like nowhere else. Varanasi has the most picturesque riverside with the banks covered with rows of stone steps that sweep down to the edge of the water. Floating past these ghats in a boat is an incomparable way to experience the river—watching an endless, colourful panorama of the joys of life and the sorrows of death on this earth.

The eternal river flows on, through the plains of Bihar, past cities like Patna that was once Pataliputra, the majestic capital of the Mauryan king Ashoka. Then it enters Bengal, nearing the end of its journey. Here the landscape is crisscrossed by a maze of rivulets and streams all heading to the sea. Slow moving, silt laden, turgid rivers full of fishing boats curve lazily around mud flats. The banks are lined by palm and coconut trees, the fields are green with rice. Ponds glisten silver by round thatched huts and dark lithe women carry shining brass water pots balanced casually against their hips.

At Kolkata, the Ganga is called the Hooghly, where ships come in from the Bay of Bengal to dock. The tired river now flows past the island of Sagardwip where the Gangasagar Mela is celebrated every winter. The ashes of King Bhagiratha's ancestors were purified here by the river goddess. Then the ocean welcomes the travel weary river into its surf tipped waves. Eternal Ganga, the beautiful daughter of the Himalayas has wandered far from home and now merges into the sea.

The image of Ganga shows a fair, beautiful woman sitting on a lotus, perched on the back a makara, a mythical river creature that seems to be a mix of a crocodile and a dolphin. She carries a pot of water in one hand. This is the *Purna Kumbha*, the pot of plenty, as the river is a symbol of fertility. Carved images of the river goddesses Ganga and Yamuna can often be seen flanking the threshold of the sanctum of temples. They are placed there as symbols of sanctity, purifying the *garbha griha* and also the worshipper who is stepping across the threshold. Some holy cities like Haridwar have temples dedicated to Ganga but people prefer to worship the river itself by touching her waters and not in a temple. They lay garlands of flowers across the water and do the *arati* of the river itself.

There is a need for a tactile worship of the river as the *Mahabharata* says, "The mere utterance of the name of the Ganga redeems the sinner. The mere sight of the Ganga amounts to a pious act. To bathe in it or to drink its waters leads to the salvation of seven generations and no sooner do the ashes of the dead touch the water, then the soul is transported to heaven." In the *Mahabharata* Ganga appears as the daughter of the Himalayas who marries Shantanu and is the mother of the patriarch of the Kurus, Bhishma.

Ganga is the daughter of the Himalayas and so she is a sister of Parvati. She is connected to all the three members of the Hindu trinity. She is said to reside in the brass pot of water held by Brahma, she is at times depicted as a consort of Vishnu and at others as a consort of Shiva. In one version of the myth of the Vamana avatar of Vishnu, when the dwarf Vamana takes the three giant steps to fool the demon Bali, at the third step his foot strikes the vault of heaven and breaks it and the Ganga pours down to earth. Another version says that Brahma poured out Ganga from his brass pot to cleanse Vishnu's feet. So the river brings the holy presence of the trinity to earth and this makes her truly sacred.

The goddess is usually depicted as a compassionate, forgiving, generous deity. Her waters are liquid *amrita*, the "sublime wine of immortality". She is Swarga-sopana-sarani, a flowing staircase to heaven. For most of the people she is simply Ganga Ma, the all accepting divine Mother. She is Samanyadhatri, the mother, sustainer and nourisher of life. And Triloka-patha-gamini, as she flows in three worlds. Her numerous names include Bhadrasoma, Gandini, Kirati (wife of Shiva), Devabhuti (coming from heaven), Harashekhara (crest of Shiva), Khapaga (flowing from heaven), Patita Pavani (purifier of the fallen) and Divyadhuni (moving the celestials).

During her descent from heaven she had flowed over the sacrificial fire of the sage Jahnu who in his rage swallowed the river. Then at the request of the gods he let her flow out again from his ear. So she is also the child of Jahnu and is called Jahnavi. Shiva holds her in his hair and so he is called Gangadhara and her son Bhishma is also called Gangeya.

The Ganga is the symbol of purity and her waters bring liberation, *moksha* to people. It is believed that her waters can never be polluted and the river forms a sacred bridge between this world and the next. Bathing in the Ganga brings liberation from the cycle of births and eases the journey to heaven. That is why a few drops of Ganga water are poured over the lips of the dying to ensure a safe passage to heaven. The river is thus deeply connected to all the rituals of death and this is found the most in Varanasi. The finest death is at Varanasi when the ashes are immersed in the river. So for centuries people have come to the city to die. All the rituals of death and memorial, funeral rites of the *shraddha*, the worship of ancestors in the *tarpana* are all performed on the ghats by the river. In Varanasi the river is a living presence like nowhere else, she is mother, protector, a healer and a final embrace.

Four

THE GHATS BY THE GANGA
Stairways to Heaven

"Ganga, her fine garments falling down.
High over her many stories of mansions.
Like a woman with her hair piled up,
And bound in a net of pearls, she bears,
Masses of clouds, shedding water in the rainy season."

—Kalidas in *'Meghadutam'* (trans. by Chandra Rajan)

When the sun rises over the Ganga in Varanasi, Surya announces his arrival with all the subtle theatre of a hero's entrance on stage. As the darkness begins to lighten, the edges of the clouds in the east are tinged with a pale pink. Slowly the palette of colours grows more vivid, as the sky deepens to a pale bluish purple and the edges of the clouds get a brush of orange. Then the sun god rides in on his seven horse chariot and the river lets him paint her waters with a shimmering silver as the tips of the ripples turn a mellow amber, the colour of a guttering oil lamp.

It is a river front like no other in the world. For centuries it has enchanted painters, inspired artists and captured the imagination of writers and poets. At dawn, if you sit on the stone steps of the Tulsi ghat what unfolds before your eyes is like a mirage from another, more ancient time. As the first sun's rays streak across the sky in the east, they slowly light up the ghats of Varanasi and reveal their classically beautiful visage. If pilgrims have come again and again to this river bank it is because of the primeval magnetism of this awesome river. They say flowing waters can cast a spell and at Kashi, one of the greatest rivers in the world can mesmerise you for life.

The western bank of the river arcs like a bow and it is lined by a fantasy world. A red gold cityscape of temple spires, the windows and balconies of mansions and minarets of mosques that reaches down to the water edge by sweeping stretches of stone steps. For a distance of five kilometres the west bank of the river is covered by these steps, with buildings rising above them. These steps are the legendary ghats of Kashi, where the world has gathered for centuries to worship the Ganga. The dream of the Hindus is to live by the river so that they can bathe in her cleansing waters every day. In medieval times the rich built their mansions and temples on the bank and then added the steps down to the edge of the waters.

As the sunshine deepens and the light hits the crescent of red sandstone ghats and the walls, balconies and arches of the buildings rising above them, for a moment you feel you are in another age and time. Sitting there it is easy to imagine Kabir or Tulsidas, even the Buddha or Guru Nanak walking along those steps to the river edge on a chilly winter's dawn. Or sheltering under a doorway as the monsoon rain pours down and the rising waters of the river lap threateningly at the edge of the temples.

The best way to savour the subtle pleasures of these ghats is to take a boat at dawn from one of the ghats, may be Tulsi, Asi or Panchganga and then tell the boatman to row close to the steps towards Dasashwamedha ghat. The visual contrast between the two banks of the river can be quite startling. On one side the river bank is an empty stretch of sand with a few lonely fishermen silhouetted against the cerulean blue bowl of the sky. Then as you turn your head you are looking at an amazing medieval city rising along the other bank, curving like a majestic amphitheatre presenting an ever changing kaleidoscope of life on its steps.

You never tire of watching this moving panorama of people and architecture unrolling lazily by your boat. Boys jump off the high stone pillars and splash in the water around the boat, lithe as seals, white teeth gleaming in the dark shiny faces. Pilgrims take their three ritual dips in the river, quickly bobbing up and down. Some ghats like Dasashwamedha and

Panchganga are crowded with people, others have a few lonely sadhus sitting still, mysteriously communing with their inner spaces. Kashi lives on these steps. Boys fly kites and play hide and seek, old women sit in the sun and gossip, milkmen bathe their cows and buffaloes, the man bent over a grinding stone would be making the intoxicant *bhang* that is sold openly in the city as it is Shiva's favourite drink. The boatmen repair their boats at one quiet ghat and another moves to the synchronised beat of the raised arms and splashing of washermen who then cover the steps with a rainbow of drying sarees and flapping clothes.

For many the true spiritual experience of a pilgrimage to Kashi lies not in its temples but along these ghats. And the deepest experience is a boat ride at dawn along the Ganga. It should start at the edge of sunrise, when the stars are still glowing dimly in the sky and the world moves in gray shadows. Tell the boatman to drift up to the middle of the river and then wait for the sun god to reveal Shiva's city. As the darkness lightens, the ghostly silhouettes of the temples and ghats will begin to loom before you. Then shadowy figures of white clad pilgrims will begin to gather at the steps waiting for Surya to appear so that they can begin their day with an auspicious prayer.

As the horizon lightens, the gray blue waters lapping around the boatman's oars will catch stray rays of light and the pilgrims will wade into the river, even in the coldest of winters. To stand chest deep in the water, raising their faces to the rising sun, offering handfuls of Gangajal as they intone that eternal *shloka* that Indians have chanted for many millenia in praise of Surya,

"Om bhur bhuvasya, tat savitur vareniam
Bhargo devasya dhimahi, dhiyo yo nah prachodayat."

The Gayatri Mantra praises the sun god saying, "Lord we behold your light that fills the three worlds and pray for your radiance to illumine our minds."

As the boat moves along the river the endless ghats flow by, there are eighty of them in Varanasi. These ghats have been mostly built in the eighteenth and nineteenth centuries and were patronised by Maratha rulers who took an active interest in reviving the city after the demolitions during the reign of Aurangzeb. They have been built by monarchs and their queens as acts of worship, as the gifts of saints and business magnates, a lowly boatman, a seller of grain and a Muslim governor of the city during Mughal times.

The ghats stand at a curve of the river where the Ganga inexplicably moves northward for a while before once more flowing to the east. They say that when the river was going past Kashi she fell in love with Shiva's beautiful home and nearly turned back to stay there. Then Bhagirath's prayers made her move on. Over the years many ghats have been shortened to create more ghats like the old Asi Ghat has been divided into Gangamahal, Tulsi, Rewa and Bhadiani and covered with steps.

Panchtirthi Yatra

Among all the ghats five have gathered the most spiritual merit and are always on the visiting list of pilgrims. These are Dasashwamedha, Asi, Adi Keshava, Panchganga and Manikarnika and they are mentioned in the *Avimukta*

Mahatmaya of the Matsya Purana. They were originally all at the points where small streams flowed into the Ganga, though now the streams are only visible at Asi, the Asi Sangam and Adi Keshava, called the Varuna Sangam. Visiting these five ghats is called the Panchtirthi Yatra.

As the *Kashi Khanda*, a treatise written in praise of Kashi says, "There, O Prince, is the very excellent 'Five Tirthas', the Panchtirthi, having bathed in which a person shall never again be born."

"First is the Asi confluence, the foremost and supreme of *tirthas*. Then there is Dasashwamedha, honoured by all the *tirthas*. Next comes the 'foot water' *tirtha* at Adi Keshava. Then there is the holy 'five rivers' of Panchanada, which destroys one's sins by simply bathing there. Beyond these four *tirthas* is the fifth, O excellent one. It is called Manikarnika, which bestows purity on the mind and senses."

"Having bathed in the five *tirthas* a person never again receives a body of five elements. Rather, he becomes the five-faced Shiva in Kashi."

The Panchtirthi Yatra takes the pilgrim all along the length of the ghats from south to north. Though one can do it by boat, it is more meritorious to perform the *yatra* by walking. At each ghat they perform the *sankalp*, the ceremony stating the intention of the pilgrim. This is usually performed with the help of a priest. For some the *yatra* is undertaken in the fulfilment of a vow, others do it desiring something but the best yatra is done *nishkama*, without desires, where the rewards are left to Shiva. It is this *nishkama yatra* that is the finest of all pilgrimages, that makes the soul truly at one with the Almighty. As the *Katha Upanishad* says with such lyrical simplicity,

"Know this,
The chariot is the body,
Intellect the charioteer, mind the reins
The senses, they say, are the steeds."

Pilgrims begin at the southernmost ghat of Asi, then move to Dasashwamedha, from there to the northernmost ghat of Adi Keshava. Then they retrace their steps to stop at Panchganga. Their *yatra* ends at holy Manikarnika and after a bath here they walk to the Kashi Vishwanath Temple for their puja. Coming out into Vishwanath Gali they drop in at the Annapurna Temple and finally stop at the shrine of Sakshi Vinayaka where Lord Ganesh as 'sakshi' or witness, records that they have completed the Panchtirthi Yatra successfully. This *yatra* is the most popular *yatra* among pilgrims and can be done in one day. Some *tirthayatris* replace the Adi Keshava with the Kedar ghat and worship at the Kedareshwar temple.

Asi Ghat

This ghat is the southernmost ghat and marks the boundary of ancient Kashi as the stream Asi flows into the Ganga here. Today this is one of the few ghats that is still an earthen embankment and has not been built over with steps. The steps begin with the Tulsi ghat that stands next to it. A crowd of boats waits by the embankment to take the pilgrims along the river. The temples visited by pilgrims here include the *lingam* of Asi Sangameshwara, and the *lingam* that stands under a peepal tree by the banks. The pool of Lolarka Kund, an ancient shrine to Surya sees a big festival every monsoon when married couples come there to ask for children. The Ganesh temple of Arka Vinayaka stands right next to the pool.

The myth of this ghat says that Durga defeated the demons Shumbh and Nishumbh here and then tiredly dropped her sword, an *asi*, that cut the channel for the Asi river. In the seventeenth century the poet Tulsidas lived on this ghat when he composed his immortal epic, *Ramcharit Manas* that retold the tale of Rama and Sita in Avadhi, the language of the people, and immediately became popular. Today the *Ramcharit Manas* is read by devotees all across north India and part of Asi ghat has been covered with stone steps and named after him. His house displays his wooden clogs and an image of Hanuman that he used to worship. Asi ghat sees a huge influx of devotees during festivals like Makar Sankranti, Mauni Amavasya and Ganga Dussehra.

Dasashwamedha Ghat

Step off your boat at the most famous ghat of all—sacred Dasashwamedha which is crowded with pilgrims from dawn to night. This is where King Divodasa performed his famous *ashvamedha yajnas* and those ten sacrifices give this ghat its special spiritual resonance. Bathing at Dasashwamedha brings *moksha*, that liberation from the cycle of births and deaths that every pilgrim is seeking. Because here as they take the three ritual dips in the water, Divodasa's merits touch them like a gentle blessing from the past.

In the *Puranas*, Dasashwamedha is called Rudrasar, the nectar of Shiva and Rudrasarovara, the lake of Rudra and the name is still used in the *mantras*. It is the largest and busiest ghat, with a broad expanse of steps always crowded with pilgrims. The present ghat was built in 1735 by the Maratha chieftain Peshwa Baji Rao. Here the *pandas* or *ghatias*, the brahmin priests who perform *pujas* on the ghats, sit waiting for the devotees on wooden *chowkis*, shaded by round reed umbrellas, with their tattered religious texts, brass and copper *puja* utensils. After their bath, worshippers do *puja* at the Shitala temple above the steps. There are three other *lingams* on the ghat that pilgrims visit—Shulatankeshwar, Shiva carrying the spear; Brahmeshwar, the lingam placed by Lord Brahma when he worshipped Shiva here and Dasashwamedheshwar, that stands within the compound of the Shitala temple and is the lingam of the ghat.

For a unique experience sit on the steps at Dasashwamedha and watch the world go by. It is always a vivid panorama of the people who have collected here drawn by the same spiritual hunger. The flower sellers sit behind golden piles of marigolds, fragrant rose and jasmine garlands and incense drifts in the air from the many small shrines lining the steps. The beggars wait beside them and their cries mingle with the call of the pilgrims intoning *mantras* and the sudden clanging of temple bells. The dazzling colours and frenetic movement is all framed by the lazily moving river and the sky above creating a living portrait of India.

The bathers stream down the steps in a dizzying movement of colours, many carrying *thalis* of flowers and incense and their faces capture the variety of our land. Silk clad Tamilians with their forehead smeared with sandalwood stand beside Gujarati villagers in clothes bright with mirrors, ebullient

Bengalis in dhotis enthusiastically join white clad Malayalis in bargaining for trinkets and brass pots of *gangajal*. For centuries Dasashwamedha has magnetically called the faithful to its steps and united this diverse land by the threads of its myths and legends, tradition and beliefs.

Every stage of the cycle of life is celebrated at this ghat. Here every Hindu ritual from a celebration of birth, marriages to funerals and the worship of ancestors is performed by the *ghatias*. Parents come with their babies and perform the *naamkaran puja*. Young boys get their heads shaved in the *mundan* and the *upanayan* ceremony of the sacred thread. Newly married couples come seeking Ganga's blessings and throw garlands on the waters. Others come to remember their ancestors by doing the *pindadaan* and *tarpana* ceremony, especially during the period of *pitripaksha*. In the middle of all the noise and bustle of people, these ceremonies are still performed with an unusual serenity, the priest's voice rising in prayers as the rituals of flowers and sandalwood, incense and lighted lamps are offered by a quiet circle of worshippers.

Arati at Dasashwamedha

As dusk falls they do an unforgettable *arati* of the river at Dasashwamedha. Take a boat and get in front of the rickety little platform standing a few feet in the water. Here, on two ghats the priests worship Ganga with incense and flowers, milk and vermilion. They create a floating *rangoli* on the water with marigold garlands, rose petals and a spray of vermilion. Then they place earthen lamps placed in floating leaf bowls around the pattern. The *arati* here follows the familiar ritual except for one difference—usually in temples the priest looks up to the face of the goddess and raises the offerings high towards it. Here he bends low towards the water, touching the river with the incense, sandalwood, waving the white mane of the whisks and flowers.

First there is the rising chant of *mantras* and then rows of lamps are lit on the steps behind the priest, placing him in a golden halo of light. These lamps are reflected in the water, multiplied into many flames and suddenly the river catches fire. Then the chanting priests fall silent and the booming drums and crashing cymbals take over. The flaring fire of the lighted camphor and the golden flicker of the many flamed oil lamp is raised high to the sky and then brought down in an arc to illumine the dark river.

People float tiny lamps in leaf boats into the water and their fragile flames dot the water like a spangled veil. Finally in the deepening darkness all you can see moving in and out of the drifting smoke is the shadowy face of the priest absorbed in his worship and the river accepting his *puja* by turning to flame reflecting the fire. Time stands still as Kashi worships her beloved river goddess.

Adi Keshava Ghat

Pilgrims now walk along the length of all the ghats to reach the northernmost ghat of Adi Keshava. This ghat is beyond the Malviya Bridge along the Rajghat Plateau which is the oldest part of Kashi. So the ghat is one of the oldest ghats of the *tirtha*. However it is not visited much by pilgrims. Some even replace Adi Keshava with the Kedar Ghat for a quicker

Panchtirthi Yatra. The Adi Keshava and the Varuna Sangam are also important stops on the more rigorous Panch Kroshi Yatra in which pilgrims walk for a distance of five *kros* and visit 108 shrines.

As the myth of Divodasa tells us, Vishnu arrived at this ghat and first washed his feet in the river before having a bath. So ancient Adi Keshava finds mention in the Puranas' list of Kashi *tirthas*. It says that Kashi was a divine body—Asi was the head, Dasashwamedha the chest, Manikarnika the navel, Panchganga the thigh and Adi Keshava the feet.

Just beyond the ghat the Varuna river flows into the Ganga and pilgrims bathe in the confluence and perform *puja* at the *lingam* of Sangameshwara, the Lord of the Sangam. The Adi Keshava temple, built by a Dewan to the Maratha chief Mahadaji Scindia has an image of Lord Vishnu in the *garbha griha*. The temple of Sangameshwara stands beside the Adi Keshava temple and has the four faced *lingam* called Brahmeshwara. The area also has two Ganesh temples, Kharva Vinayaka and Rajaputra Vinayaka.

Panchganga Ghat

This is the most majestic ghat of all, with its broad sweeping steps and rows of riverside shrines. Tradition says that the five rivers that give the ghat its name are supposed to flow into the Ganga here, though only the Ganga can be seen. These rivers are Dhutapapa (cleansed of sin), Kirana (like the rays of the sun), Dharmanada (the river of Dharma), Saraswati, Yamuna and Ganga. So bathing at this ghat means bathing in the sacred waters of five rivers.

Once this ghat had a famous temple called Bindu Madhav. It is said that a sage Agni Bindu performed many years of *tapas* here and when Vishnu wanted to give him a boon, he begged that Vishnu should always reside here for his devotees. Vishnu agreed and also said that the temple would bear both his name, Madhav and the sage's name Bindu. The month of Kartik is considered the most auspicious at this ghat when oil lamps are lit and placed inside small woven baskets and hung from the end of long bamboo poles to pray for the peace of the soul of ancestors. These lamps are called *akash deep*, sky lamps and are lit during the festival of Devadeepa Mallika. On Kartik Purnima night a tall stone lamp with a thousand wicks that stands at the top of the ghat is also lit and glows across the river in a fiery benediction from Vishnu.

The ghat has a distinctive row of open cubicles built under the steps, right at the edge of the water. These are visible only when the water level is low. Some of them are small shrines where the bathers can do *puja* while still standing in the river. Sadhus often occupy the empty cubicles and sit meditating peacefully, away from the noise and bustle of the ghat above their heads. Another rather amusing sight every morning and evening are the wrestlers doing their exercises on the steps. There are a number of wrestling *akharas* in the locality and these muscle bound men, often surrounded by a throng of admirers, lift huge wooden weights and do sit ups here before plunging into the river for a quick breather.

Once this ghat had the legendary Bindu Madhav temple, built in the sixteenth century by Raja Man Singh of Amber, a trusted courtier of Akbar who encouraged a revival of Kashi. His finance minister Raja Todar Mal built the Adi Vishweshwara temple but Man Singh's temple far surpassed it in magnificence. These temples did not last long as both were demolished by the orders of Akbar's great-grandson Aurangzeb in the next century.

The Italian traveller Tavernier saw this temple and marvelled at its size and architecture. He called it the 'great pagoda' that was shaped like a cross with a tower at each end and a gigantic *shikhara* rising from the centre over the *garbha griha*. It was such a large structure that it stretched over the Panchganga ghat and then covered the next ghat, now called Rama ghat. The temple of the goddess Mangala Gauri stood within its precincts. Tavernier describes the tall image of Bindu Madhav in the sanctum being clad in silks and covered with precious jewels. The poet Tulsi Das who was fortunate enough to see these edifices wrote in praise of the Bindu Madhav image,

> "You dwell on the bank of the gods' river in a choice temple
> Blessed are the eyes of those men who have the sight of you."

Panchganga is rich with history and legend. The *bhakti* poet and saint Kabir received his *mantra* from his guru Ramananda at this ghat. Kabir belonged to a low caste and was thus not allowed to get a *mantra*. He knew that Ramananda came to Panchganga for his morning bath, so one day, before dawn, he lay down on the steps on his path. Ramananda coming down the steps nearly tripped over him and muttered "Ram! Ram!" and Kabir took these words as his guru's *mantra*. The *ashrams* of the sages Ramananda, Tailangaswami and Ballabhacharya are all located near this ghat.

One of the most beautiful poems written by a citizen of Kashi in praise of the Ganga is *Ganga Lahari* by Jagannath and his story is also woven with this ghat. Jagannath was patronised by Shahjahan's son Dara Shikoh. At the Mughal court he fell in love with a Muslim woman and because of this he was declared impure by the brahmins and ostracised by the people of Kashi. Jagannath decided that he would ask Ganga to purify him and wrote,

> "I come without refuge to you, giver of sacred rest
> I come a fallen man to you, uplifter of all
> I come undone by pain to you, the perfect physician
> I come, my heart filled with thirst to you,
> O ocean of sweet wine
> Do with me whatever you will."

One day Jagannath and his beloved sat on the top steps of the Panchganga ghat and he began to sing the fifty two verses of *Ganga Lahiri*. With each verse the waters rose to cover one step and at the end the river swept them away.

After demolishing the Bindu Madhav temple Aurangzeb decided to build a giant mosque in its place. A mosque that would dominate the river front and stamp Kashi with the power of his bigotry. So the gigantic Alamgir mosque was built and its forbidding walls look down at the colourful throng of pilgrims with grim disapproval and the dome is visible from faraway. Aurangzeb wanted the two minarets to be the tallest structures in the city. However the minarets became so unstable that they had to be shortened again and again.

Today the truncated minarets look rather incongruous against the huge dome behind them and the local people still call the mosque 'Beni Madhav ka dharhara'—the ruins of Beni Madhav. Even after three centuries the temple has not been forgotten. The present Bindu Madhav temple is a small shrine in a lane behind the Alamgir mosque. Pilgrims doing the Panchtirthi yatra visit this temple and also the shrines to Mangala Gauri, Surya, Mayukhaditya and Gabhastishvara.

Manikarnika Ghat

No other ghat captures one's imagination like fiery Manikarnika, it speaks of life and death, creation and destruction in the same breath and offers liberation and peace to the faithful. Manikarnika is like Kashi, wise in her knowledge of human frailties and like its god, it is tolerant and forgiving. Among its stark images of sorrow and death Manikarnika still offers a quiet requiem to the souls of the departed. Manikarnika, means a jewelled earring and Kashi with its typical contrary humour gave this poetic name to a cremation ground.

This is the ghat that has somehow become the symbol of the riverfront of Kashi. During daytime it is wreathed in smoke from the many burning pyres on its steps. After night falls the fires can be seen from far, a glow of orange against the dark night sky. They say the fires have not gone out for centuries at sacred Manikarnika

In Kashi they say, "Drishyo Vishveshwaro nityam, snatavya Manikarnika", everyday you should do the darshan of Vishveshwara and bathe at Manikarnika. This ghat is the final stop of the Panchtirthi pilgrim. It is the sacred fifth, the centre of the holy grouping of five in Hindu symbolism and so Manikarnika is the centre of both creation and destruction.

Creation through the sacred pool that was dug here by Vishnu. The cremation ground is the kingdom of Shiva as Tarakeshwar, the god of death and liberation. As Diana Eck writes, "Both the waters of creation and the fires of destruction join in the aura of sanctity that pervades Manikarnika."

The Manikarnika Kund, is also called Chakrapushkarini Kund because Vishnu dug this lotus pool with his chakra. The kund is a square stepped pool right above the steps. The many myths around the kund are all woven around a *manikarnika*, a jewelled earring, in some stories worn by Parvati and in others by Shiva himself. It is the fall of this divine earring that gives this pool its name. The *Kashi Khanda*, tells this myth, as translated by Diana Eck:

"One day Shiva and Shakti, living in the Forest of Bliss, began to think how fine it would be to have another being who would create the world, bear its burdens and protect it. The two of them would not have to worry about such matters and could devote themselves to the granting of liberation. Thus, they created Vishnu, beautiful and worthy, the very epitome of all good qualities. They instructed him to create everything on earth, according to the plan of the sacred Vedas."

"Receiving this command, Vishnu immediately set himself on the path of severe austerities. Digging there with his discus, called a *chakra*, Hari made a beautiful lotus pond, called a *Pushkarini* and he filled it up with water from the sweat of his own limbs. Like a stone, he sat there, on the banks of the Chakrapushkarini Pool and performed fierce austerities for five lakh years."

"One day, Shiva and Shakti came that way and saw him there, aflame with the heat of his austerities. Shiva hailed him, and told him to choose a boon. Vishnu's only wish was to live forever in the presence of the Supreme Shiva. Hearing this, Shiva shook with sheer delight at the great devotion of Vishnu, and his jewelled earring, the *manikarnika*, fell from his ear into the waters of the pool. Shiva granted Vishnu's request and added another boon of his own: This place, the Chakrapushkarini would now be known as Manikarnika, the 'Jewelled Earring'."

Another version of this myth found in the Shiva Purana also includes Brahma and explains the reason for the building of the city. Amusingly, here as in the earlier myth the traditional story of creation is changed and the destroyer Shiva is also both creator and preserver. He is the true celestial mover in the whole drama of creation and he is superior to Brahma and often commands Vishnu to do specific tasks.

It says, "The unmanifest, attributeless One, Brahman, produced a second being, called Shiva and possessing attributes. Shiva then split into two, becoming male and female, Shiva and Shakti. They, in turn, created Purusha, who was Vishnu and Prakriti, his consort. These two, Purusha and Prakriti were commanded to perform austerities in order to create the universe. But where should they practice their discipline? As yet there was no place in the void."

"The Supreme Shiva then created a beautiful city, radiant and auspicious, five *kroshas* in extent. Vishnu, the Purusha, then sat in that place, labouring and heating himself in austerities. From his labour, water began to flow from his body and out over the face of the void. When Vishnu saw the water, he shook his head in wonder, and his earring fell into the water. Thus, it became known as the 'Jewelled Earring'

Manikarnika. Finally, the water became so extensive that the city of the five *kroshas* began to float, supported by the trident of the attributeless Shiva. Vishnu slept there on the waters, and brought forth Brahma and the Cosmic Egg from his navel in order to produce creation. Shiva then took Kashi down from his trident and released it into the mortal world, but when that world dissolves again Shiva upholds the radiant Kashi on his trident."

The pretty idea of a piece of jewellery falling into a pool obviously inspired the mythmakers of ancient times because in a third version Shiva and Parvati both bathed in Vishnu's pool. Then during their bath Shiva's crest jewel, the *mani*, and Parvati's earring, a *karnika* fell into the pool. Scholars feel that the word *mani* is often connected to *nagas* who are supposed to guard treasures and so this may have been a place of snake worship. Kashi itself has innumerable stones carved with *nagas* strewn around its temple precincts and *naga* worship is still very prevalent as proven by the popularity of the festival of Naga Panchami.

The imagery of the earring is tied to the boon of liberation in one version where Vishnu says that just as the earring was freed, made 'mukta' from Shiva's ear, similarly this should be a *tirtha* where people can be freed from the coils of mortal life. Kind Vishnu got the boon of *moksha* for everyone and you do not have to be a great *yogi* or sage to gain liberation at Manikarnika.

Then after granting all these boons, Shiva added one of his own—he made all creation the kingdom of Vishnu. So as at Adi Keshava, at Manikarnika Vishnu is also worshipped by the devotees in this city of Shiva. They say that as the *tirtha* of the *tirthas*, the emanations at Manikarnika are so strong that even the other *tirthas* of the land come to bathe here to wash away the sins they have collected from pilgrims and the gods come here to bathe every day.

The Panchtirthi Yatra is not performed in the monsoons as the river rises and floods this ghat and covers the Manikarnika Kund. So every year after the monsoons the pool has to be cleared of accumulated silt. In a decoration ceremony the people call 'shringar', the pool is cleared, the walls of the buildings around are painted again and covered with brilliantly coloured murals telling the myth of the pool.

At Manikarnika pilgrims perform puja to Shiva, Vishnu and the Devi. Vishnu is worshipped at his footprints, the Charanapaduka, set in a circular slab of marble, inside an open pavilion. At one time the royalty of Kashi were cremated next to this shrine. Then they head for the Tarakeshwara temple. As Tarakeshwara, Shiva is the divine boatman who rows the souls of the dead across the river to heaven, all the while singing the Taraka Mantra of liberation. Another temple is of Manikarnikeshwara where the *lingam* is placed underground. The Goddess is known here as Manikarni Devi. She is an ancient goddess and finds mention in the *Linga Purana* and *Kashi Khanda*. Manikarni Devi is worshipped while bathing in the pool and it is she who presides over the *shringara* ceremonies, when the waters are covered with flowers and an arti is performed.

The cremation ghat is actually the adjoining row of steps to the Manikarnika ghat and this ghat is not visited during the Panchtirthi Yatra. This area is supervised by the Doms, the traditional caste who run cremation grounds. They tend the ever burning fire from which a flame is taken to light a pyre. They also offer the ashes to the river later. Scholars say that the Harishchandra ghat cremation ground is older but over the years Manikarnika has gained greater sanctity. In old texts this cremation ghat is called Jalasai ghat but nowadays it is connected to the holy pool and also called Manikarnika. The cremation ground is considered very sacred and significant by *tantriks* who can be seen meditating here and during the *amavasya* night in the month of Kartik they come from faraway places to meditate here.

The burning ghat came into being in the eighteenth century. Originally it was called Rajabhallabh ghat with the Jaleshwar ghat next to it. In 1760 the mother of a Lala Kashmiri Lal died and he was the treasurer of Nawab Safdarjung of Avadh. The Lala was deeply angered by the avaricious demands of the doms of Harishchandra ghat and decided to cremate his mother on Rajabhallabh ghat. It was a sacred spot next to the Brahmanala stream with the *kund* nearby. Since then cremations have taken place here.

After Manikarnika the pilgrim now moves away from the river and heads into the city, walking down the narrow lanes that connect it to the Vishwanath Gali. First they stop at the Siddhi Vinayaka temple, then enter Kashi Vishwanath and perform *puja*. Coming out they drop in at the Annapurna temple to pay their obeisance to the goddess of plenty and then the final stop is at the Sakshi Vinayaka temple where Ganesha as the witness, makes note that the pilgrim has truly completed the great Panchtirthi Yatra.

Kubernath Sukul, a scholar of the city, in his book *Varanasi Vaibhav,* gives a list of ghats and temples pilgrims visit during the Panchtirthi Yatra:

1. Asi ghat – Asi Madhav, Trivikrama, Asi Sangameshwara, Lolarka Kund, Arka Vinayaka.
2. Dasashwamedha ghat – Dasashwamedeshwar, Vandi Devi, Shultankeshwar, Adi Varaha, Someshwar, Dalbhyeshwar, Prayag Madhav.
3. Varuna Sangam – Padodak Tirtha, Adi Keshava, Sangameshwar, Kharva Vinayaka, Keshavaditya, Gyan Keshava, Nakshatreshwar, Vedeshwar.
4. Panchganga ghat – Bindu Madhav, Gabhasteeshwar, Mangala Gauri.
5. Manikarnika ghat – Manikarni Devi, Siddha Vinayaka, Manikarnikeshwar.
6. Vishweshwar temple, Annapurna temple, Gyan Vapi well.

Kedar Ghat & Kedareshwar Temple

Among the other ghats that are popular with worshippers is Kedar ghat that was renovated by the Maharaja of Vijianagram. This is one of the oldest ghats of Kashi and even has its own book of praise in the *Kashi Kedar Mahatmya*. It is one of the first temples mentioned in the Puranic *mahatmyas* and in the *Kashi Khanda* it has a full chapter devoted to its praise. It has the oldest Shiva lingam in Kashi and is respected as an elder of Lord Vishweshwar of the Kashi Vishwanath temple. The people of the city will tell you that like a generous elder brother, Kedar allowed Vishweshwar to become the pre-eminent deity of the city. The temple also managed to survive the destruction during the reign of Aurangzeb and so the structure is much older than other temples in Varanasi. Another proof of its ancient history is the small pool by the steps called Gauri Kund that is also called Adi Manikarnika.

Kedar means a field and the *Mahatmya* says, "It is known as the field where the crop of liberation grows." This ghat is said to be the namesake of the famous Shiva shrine of Kedarnath in the Himalayas, that stands beside the Mandakini river. The Kedarnath *lingam* is one of the twelve sacred *jyotirlingams*. The Pandava brothers worshipped Kedarnath on their journey of atonement after the battle at Kurukshetra.

The Kedar temple is a river temple standing on top of the flight of steps of the ghat. Its red and white striped walls are easy to spot from a distance. It sits on top of one of the three hills of the city that are called the three prongs of the trident of Shiva. This temple is very popular with South Indian and Bengali worshippers who bathe in the river and then carry up brass pots of water to perform the *abhishekha* of the *lingam*. The *lingam* is a rough rock with a white line running through it and is believed to be a *swayambhu lingam*, a self manifest image.

The myth of the temple says that a king named Mandhatri gave up all his possessions and began to worship Shiva in Kashi. Every day Mandhatri using his yogic powers would mentally travel to the Himalayan Kedar shrine and worship Shiva there and then return to Kashi. However as he grew old this daily pilgrimage became harder for him to perform and Shiva told him to eat first before making the pilgrimage. So he cooked a plate of *khichri*, a lentil and rice dish, and went looking for someone to share it with. Shiva himself appeared before him in the guise of a *sadhu* and when Mandhatri cut the *khichri* in half it turned into a stone *lingam* with a white line running in the middle and Shiva revealed himself to him and accepted his worship. The *Kashi Khanda* says, "What fruit one gets from climbing the snowy mountains and seeing Kedar, that one obtains seven-fold by seeing Kedar in Kashi."

Other Ghats

Many of the other ghats may not be important for religious reasons but have their own character and interesting legends. A twentieth century saint built a ghat named after her as the Mata Anandmayee ghat. Built in 1944, a temple and a girl's school stand on top of the steps. Many ghats are patronised by people from different regions, like the Jains come to Bachchharaj ghat where the saint Suparshvanath was born and on the Jain ghat there is a notice on the steps prohibiting fishing. Gujaratis come and stay around Sankatha ghat, Maharashtrians patronise Bhonsla and Ram ghats, South Indians and Bengalis come to Kedar ghat.

Nishadhraj and Nishadh ghats are boatmen's ghats and at Nishadhraj the boatmen have their own temple. The washermen work at Prabhu and Pandey ghats. Chait Singh ghat was built by Balwant Singh, the Raja of Banaras and in 1781 his descendant Chait Singh fought and lost a battle with Warren Hastings at the fortress above this ghat. Now part of this fort has been donated to the two Naga sadhu sects of the Niranjani and Nirvani akharas who have their monasteries and temples here. The Juna Akhara is at Hanuman ghat where the sixteenth century saint Swami Vallabhacharya used to stay.

Some say the cremation ground of the Harishchandra ghat is where the legendary king Harishchandra worked as a dom after he had lost all his possessions though scholars feel this is a comparitively new ghat. Raja Man Singh of Amber who built the Bindu Madhav temple also built the two ghats of Mansarovar and Man Mandir. On top of the Man Mandir ghat his descendant Raja Jai Singh II built an observatory in the eighteenth century. An interesting shrine dedicated to sixty four *yoginis*, the Chaunsath Yogini temple, stands above the Chaunsathhi ghat. Rani Ahilyabai of Indore who rescued the Vishweshwar *lingam* and rebuilt the Kashi Vishwanath temple also built the Ahilyabai ghat in the eighteenth century. Rajendra Prasad ghat is named after India's first president, it was once called Ghora ghat as a nearby market sold horses.

When Baija Bai, the wife of Daulat Rao Sindhia built the Sindhia ghat most of it collapsed into the river. Mir ghat was built in the eighteenth century by a Muslim governor of the city, Faujdar Mir Rustam Ali. The Devi shrine of the Vishalakshi temple here is very popular with pilgrims from the south. On Lalita ghat is the Lalita Devi temple built by the kings of Nepal in wood and brick in a Nepalese style of architecture. The Jatar ghat was once called Chor ghat, a thief's ghat as the bathers often found their possessions vanishing here! At Gai ghat people come to bathe and perform *prayashchitta*, the *puja* of atonement if they have killed a cow. Ghats have also been built by ordinary people, like Chawki ghat was built by a man who sold roasted grain. One of the oldest ghats is Raj ghat next to the Malaviya Bridge where archaeologists have found artefacts going back to the third century BC.

Over the years the number of ghats has varied as larger ghats got divided or some important ghats subsumed nearby ones. For those interested in numbers and names the names of the 80 ghats are given here. We are moving from the south to the north and technically the southernmost ghat is the local ghat of Nagwa, though for the pilgrim the sacred ghats only begin at Asi at the Asi Sangam.

From Asi Ghat to Dasashwamedha Ghat—

1. Nagwa. 2. Asi. 3. Ganga Mahal (one). 4. Riwa. 5. Tulsi. 6. Bhadaini. 7. Janaki. 8. Mata Anandamoyee. 9. Bachchharaj. 10. Jain. 11. Nishadraj. 12. Prabhu. 13. Panchkoti. 14. Chait Singh. 15. Niranjani. 16. Mahanirvani. 17. Shivala. 18. Gullariya. 19. Dandi. 20. Hanuman. 21. Karnataka. 22. Harishchandra. 23. Laali. 24. Vijiayanagram. 25. Kedar. 26. Chauki. 27. Kshemeshwar. 28. Mansarovar. 29. Narad. 30. Raja. 31. Pandey. 32. Digapatiya. 33. Chaunsathhi. 34. Ranamahal. 35. Darbhanga. 36. Munshi. 37. Ahilyabai. 38. Shitala (one). 39. Dasashwamedh.

From Prayag Ghat to Adi Keshav Ghat—

40. Prayag. 41. Rajendraprasad. 42. Man Mandir. 43. Varahi. 44. Tripura Bhairavi. 45. Meer. 46. Lalita. 47. Jalshain. 48. Manikarnika. 49. Sindhia. 50. Sankata. 51. Gangamahal (two). 52. Bhonsla. 53. Agnishwar. 54. Ganesh. 55. Mehta. 56. Ram. 57. Jataar. 58. Gwalior. 59. Balaji. 60. Panchganga. 61. Durga. 62. Brahma. 63. Bundiparkota. 64. Shitala (two). 65. Lal. 66. Hanumangarhi. 67. Gai. 68. Badrinarayan.

69. Trilochan. 70. Gola. 71. Nandishwar. 72. Shuka. 73. Teliyanala. 74. Naya. 75. Prahlad. 76. Nishad. 77. Rani. 78. Raj. 79. Khirki. 80. Adi Keshava.

Five

TEMPLES OF VARANASI
A City of Shrines

*"For Kabir, the mind is Mathura
And the face is Kashi
The body is the gate to Brahman
Where the divine light can be seen."*

—Kabir, fourteenth century Bhakti poet.

Temples and wayside shrines are woven into the life of the people of Kashi. Every morning you walk to the nearby ghat to take a dip in the river and then carry back a brass pot of gangajal for your favourite, Shiva-Shankar-Maheshwar-Mahadev. It is poured over the Shivalingam standing in a corner of the ghat or another in the sanctum of a tiny temple hidden in a forgotten corner of the dark medieval *gali*. May be on the way back you dip a quick namaskar to benign Ganesha set into a niche in the wall and covered in orange vermilion or drop a few flower petals at the feet of a Devi in her dark *garbha griha*. In Kashi the deities wait at every turn of the serpentine lanes and as they say, even the pebbles are holy in Kashi.

It is impossible to count the number of temples in Varanasi but some say there are more than two thousand of them. Some are always crowded with pilgrims, many others are just the haunt of the local people and some that are forgotten except for a few days every year. It is these temples and the ghats that have provided a source of livelihood to the citizens since time immemorial. From the *pandas*, the rickshawallas, and food shop owners to the weavers, boatmen and tourist guides, the temples are crucial to their lives. They have also been a source of creativity to the singers, musicians, dancers, painters and craftsmen of the *tirtha*. For instance, Kashi's weavers began by weaving the silk for the deities and priests and now it is the city's largest industry.

A visit to a temple is a spiritual journey that needs a preparation of both the mind and the body. The ritual of the puja is called *manastirtha*, a 'pilgrimage of the mind' whose 'deep clean water is truth'. You get up at dawn, bathe, wear fresh clothes and still fasting, you walk to the temple. Then buying the offerings of flowers, fruits, vermilion, incense and sweets from the shops at the gateways you enter the precinct of the temple. Leaving your shoes outside, you walk barefoot up the flight of stairs, through the corridors, the various pillared halls to the other end of the precinct where the small sanctum sanctorum is placed. This long walk, usually done in silence is the time when the mind is emptied of all stray thoughts and concentrated on prayers.

There are specific rituals that you follow at each temple. At the Shiva temple you offer prayers at the figure of the Nandi bull, that stands at the main doorway. A temple to a goddess may have a holy tree, another a sacred pillar. A Vishnu temple will have a figure of his vehicle Garuda. There are smaller shrines to minor deities around the sanctum and you worship them all with a few flower petals, a dot of sandalwood paste or *kumkum*. Then you circle the sanctum clockwise, doing the *pradakshina*.

Finally you reach the doorway of the sanctum, the *garbha griha*, inside the deity stands in a dark, starkly simple room, lit by flickering oil lamps. The priest who stands at the door will carry your offerings inside as you reach up and ring the bells at the door to catch the attention of a busy god. While intoning the *mantras*, the priest will touch the offerings of flowers and sweets to the deity's feet, light the incense and wave it before the god and then the offerings are returned to you as *prasada*—consecrated by the acceptance of the god. During this *puja* the communion is directly between the worshipper and the worshipped, as each devotee prays directly to the deity and the experience is unique to each one of them.

The more formal rituals of *puja* that are performed by the brahmin priests of the temple are like the consecration of a monarch. The deity is the king of all kings, the temple is his palace and the image is often placed on a throne, the *simhasan*, the lion's seat. It is bathed in perfumed water and then anointed with sandalwood paste, dressed in gorgeous garments and adorned with jewels. Vishnu may wear a crown of gold, Durga or Annapurna will have diamonds glittering at her throat and neck but ascetic Shiva is usually quite happy with a simple garland of his favourite scarlet hibiscus and fresh, green, bilva leaves.

The ceremony of the *puja* follows a specific order. Beginning at dawn, the *puja* is performed many times during the day. The five main *pujas* usually performed at Shiva temples are *mangala arti* at dawn, *bhog* at noon, *saptarishi* at dusk, *shringara* in the night and *shayan* at midnight. The most auspicious pujas are the dawn, noon and dusk pujas. The deity is offered fragrant sandalwood paste, flowers and incense. Then as it is fanned by fly whisks, burning camphor purifies the air and the cleansing fire is offered as the many flamed *arti* lamp is raised to illumine the face of the deity. Finally fruits and sweets, even cooked dishes are offered. The burning camphor and the *arti* lamp are carried outside and devotees reach out to feel the heat with their right palm and touch their heads to gather the blessings.

The holy water is sprinkled over their bent heads as the priest intones 'Om Shanti!' peace be to all, intoning that gentle *mantra* that says,

"Peaceful be heaven, peaceful the earth.
Peaceful the broad space between.
Peaceful for us be the running waters.
Peaceful the plants and herbs...
May peace prevail, happiness prevail!
May everything for us be peaceful!
Om Shanti! Om Shanti! Om Shanti!"

There are fifteen forms of puja and each ritual has a name. First the idol is offered a seat, *asana* and then formally welcomed with the chant of the *swagata*. The feet are washed, often with *panchamrita*, a mixture of the five elements of milk, yoghurt, ghee, sugar and honey and this is later offered to devotees. Water is offered in the ritual of *arghya* and it is sipped in the *achamana*. The deity is bathed, in the *snana* ritual and dressed with *vasana-bhushana*, clothes and jewellery and a mirror held before it.

Then the ritual of welcome begins. Sandalwood paste, vermilion, flowers, incense, camphor and fire in the *aarti* and finally the food called *naivedya* is offered. Then there is a second offering of water for the deity to wash its mouth and all the while there is the recital of Vedic hymns and *mantras*, the ringing of bells and blowing of conches. The priests end the ceremony with a final obeisance by lying prostrate on the floor in the *namaskriya*.

During a *tirthyatra* to Kashi, pilgrims visit the shrines of just about every important deity in the Hindu pantheon. Varanasi-Kashi may be Shiva's earthly home but then this generous volatile god welcomes all the deities to his favourite city. So everyone from Surya, Vishnu, all the planets, the many aspects of the Devi, Ganesh, demi-gods like *bhairavas* and *yoginis* and even saints and poets receive the worship of people here. It is a city that celebrates every aspect of this vibrant, many hued faith that we call Hinduism.

As the myth of Divodasa tells it, every god, *bhairava*, *yaksha* or *yogini* sent to Kashi by Shiva fell in love with the city and remained there. Generous Kashi worships all of them with prayers and flowers but its heart belongs to Shiva. His presence permeates the *tirtha*, from rows of *lingams* under a tree or beside the steps of a ghat to temples in every lane. Shiva's topknotted visage stares out of paintings on the walls, beside the whitewashed doorways of houses and hoardings on the streets. And the city has one of the most sacred shrines to Shiva in the Kashi Vishwanath temple.

Varanasi temples range from the quiet *mandirs* in the lanes where the local people go, small wayside shrines in forgotten corners of the city to the mammoth temples with soaring *shikharas* that are always crowded with devotees. It is for the devotee to choose where they feel the call to prayer—at the *lingam* sheltered under a tree by the ghat steps or the busy courtyard of the Kashi Vishwanath temple. Then all the important places of pilgrimage are supposed to have their symbolic presence here, so you can perform a *tirthayatra* of the whole land while staying in Kashi.

The Buddha walked through the lanes of Kashi before going to Sarnath. A king of Kashi fought in the battle at Kurukshetra. The Mauryan king Asoka built a stupa there. For a *tirthasthana* that traces its history back to the most ancient times of the epics and even before, Kashi should have had some of the most venerable temples in the country. Sadly none of its existing temples can trace their history back beyond the eighteenth century.

When the first Muslim invasions took place in the twelfth century, the temples of the land possessed legendary wealth and were also the strongest symbols of the religion of the people. They immediately became the irresistible targets of the invaders who swept in to destroy and plunder. Then all through the medieval period Muslim kings from Qutubuddin Aibak, Razia Sultan to the Sharqi nawabs of Jaunpur targeted the temples of Varanasi. The final and most devastating assault was in the seventeenth century when the devastation wrecked by Aurangzeb left nothing of ancient Kashi standing. Most of the present temples in the city were built in the eighteenth century by the Maratha rulers who rose to power over the ruins of the Mughal Empire.

Just like its temples, Varanasi's social and religious history too became buried somewhere in the rubble. The records of most of its temples have vanished and what remains are a melange of fading memories of names of temples and legends that talk of famous shrines built by great people. Much is lost in Kashi but this great survivor has risen again and again. It has built its temples, revived its faith and braced for the next assault. For six hundred years Kashi has survived in defiance of all bigotry. Today in triumph its temples reverberate to the sound of conch shells and bells as the chant of *mantras* rise to the sky. Eternal Kashi still celebrates its beloved gods and goddesses in its temples and sings its love for its mother river on the ghats.

The Shiva Lingams of Kashi

Some say there are forty two important Shivalingams in Kashi, some are *swayambhu* and others are *jyotirlingams*. However many of those listed in ancient texts like the *Kashi Khanda* and *Kashi Rahasya* can no longer be located after their temples were demolished.

Among the forty two the fourteen most important ancient Shivalingams, as listed in the *Kashi Khanda* are:

1. Omkareshwar, a *jyotirlingam*.
2. Trilochana, the 'Three eyed Shiva'.
3. Mahadeva, the 'Great Lord'.
4. Krittivaseshwara, the 'Lord who wears the elephant hide'.
5. Ratneshwara, 'Lord of Jewels', established by Parvati's father Himalaya.
6. Chandreshwara, 'Lord of the moon', established by Soma, the moon god.
7. Kedareshwara, a *jyotirlingam*, at Kedar ghat.
8. Dharmeshwara, the 'Lord of Dharma', established by Yama, god of death.
9. Vireshwara, the 'Hero's Lord', a *swayambhu lingam*.
10. Kameshwara, the 'Lord of Desire', established by the sage Durvasas.
11. Vishwakarmeshwara, established by the celestial architect, Vishwakarma.
12. Manikarnikeshwara, 'Lord of the Manikarnika ghat'.
13. Avimukteshwara, a *jyotirlingam*, now inside the Kashi Vishwanath temple
14. Vishweshwara, 'Lord of the World', the deity in the Kashi Vishwanath temple.

Nava Durga & Nava Gauri:

Kashi is as much Shiva's as Parvati's earthly home. So there is a strong presence of the goddess here and the Vishalakshi temple is considered a *devi pitha*. The worship of Devi goes on with that of Shiva throughout the year. There are nine Durgas and nine Gauris worshipped in Kashi and women also do a *yatra* of these deities.

The Nava Durgas are:

1. Shailaputri. 2. Brahmacharini. 3. Chitraghanta. 4. Kushmanda. 5. Skanda Mata. 6. Katyayani. 7. Kalaratri. 8. Mahagauri. 9. Siddhidatri

The Nava Gauris are:

1. Mukhanirmalika. 2. Jyeshtha. 3. Saubhagya. 4. Shringara. 5. Vishalakshi. 6. Lalita. 7. Bhavani 8. Mangala. 9. Mahalakshmi

Kashi Vishwanath Temple

There are four *lingams* in Kashi that claim to be *jyotirlingams* – Omkareshwara, Kedareshwar, Avimukteshwar and Vishweshwar. Tradition says that there were temples dedicated to all four within the *tirtha*. Also as Kashi stands on three hills that are said to be the prongs of Shiva's trident, there are three *lingams* that anchor each region, Omkara in the north, Kedara in the south and Vishweshwara in the centre. (for the Kedareshwara temple see chapter on Ghats).

In the years when the city faced frequent onslaughts from Muslim armies these shrines were often destroyed and somewhere in the past the ancient temples of Omkareshwar and Avimukteshwar have vanished. The temple to Kedareshwar still stands above Kedar ghat but the Avimukteshwara *lingam* was shifted into the precinct of the Kashi Vishwanath temple and over the years has lost out to the rising popularity of the *lingam* of Vishwanatha. Today it is one of the subsidiary shrines in the main courtyard of the Kashi Vishwanath temple.

Kashi Vishwanath is said to stand on the middle of the three hills of Varanasi and it has been the reigning deity of Kashi for at least a millenium. In the ancient texts the names Vishweshwara and Vishwantha are often used interchangeably. The Kashi Vishwanath temple is located in the heart of a maze of lanes called the Vishwanath Gali. The narrow serpentine Vishwanath Gali is lined by shops selling everything from brass *puja* utensils to flowers, textiles, trinkets and toys and it is always crowded with a surging mass of pilgrims heading for the temple. Unlike the generously proportioned temples of the south with their series of *mandapas*, soaring *gopura* gateways and high *shikharas* silhouetted against the sky, this temple is not architecturally impressive. As a matter of fact, being tucked inside a narrow lane, most of the building is hidden from view. It may not have the architectural splendour one expects from such an important shrine but this space is resonant with great sanctity and echoes to many ancient traditions. And it is this spirit of the place that still draws pilgrims from every corner of the land.

In many ways, the history of the Vishwanath temple reflects the history of the city it presides over. A tale of destruction and rebirth and destruction once again. The original Vishweshwar temple fell to the armies of Qutubuddin Aibak in 1194. Razia Sultan built a mosque at that site in the next century, so Vishweshwara was shifted into a new temple. Then in the fourteenth and fifteenth centuries the temples of Kashi were attacked a number of times during the reigns of Firuz Shah Tughlak, Mahmud Shah Sharqi of Jaunpur and Sikander Lodi and it is hard to trace the history of the temple through these tumultuous times.

In the Mughal period, the last temple to stand at this site was called Adi Vishweshwar built in 1585 by the poet Narayan Bhatta with the patronage of Akbar's finance minister Raja Todar Mal. Some texts call it the Mokshavilas temple as there was such a shrine here during the reign of Harshavardhana in the Seventh century. The Chinese traveller Hiuen Tsang describes a Mokshavilas temple with an image made of copper and not a *lingam* in the *garbha griha*. The temple is said to have rivalled in grandeur the Bindu Madhav temple built at the same time by Raja Man Singh at Panchganga Ghat. It was spread over a large area with its *garbha griha* surrounded by eight *mandapas*—the traditional pavilions that lead into the sanctum. The *garbha griha* was topped by nine *shikharas* and the *shikharas* were topped by gold *kalashas*.

The Shivalingam enshrined in that temple was called Vishweshwar. The *mandapas* were used for entertainment and the display of treasures like jewellery, gold and silver vessels, palanquins and howdahs. The outside walls were kept plain and not decorated with carvings so as not to anger the Muslim rulers. The *lingam* was placed on a gold base and protected by a railing. There were four antechambers around the *garbha griha* where the images of other deities were placed. However the history of this temple was very short as in less than a century, in 1669, Aurangzeb's armies demolished both the temples of Bindu Madhav and Adi Vishweshwara and replaced them with mosques. Here the Gyan Vapi mosque was built over the ruins. Even today the Nandi bull from the old temple sits before the mosque.

Vishwanath rose again only in the next century when in 1777 the present temple was built by Ahilyabai Holkar, the queen of Indore. The temple was built in the classical north Indian *nagara* style with multiple spires and shrines placed around a courtyard. It was built next to the Gyan Vapi mosque and the Vishweshwara *lingam*, which had been hidden in the Gyan Vapi well, was retrieved and once again enshrined in the *garbha griha*. The sanctum is topped by *shikharas* originally covered in copper that were plated in gold by Maharaja Ranjit Singh of Punjab in 1835. It took 820 kilos of gold and the spires gleaming in the sun give the shrine the name of the Golden Temple. Warren Hastings is said to have financed the building of the music gallery, the *naubat khana*. In 1839 Lord Irwin, the Viceroy of India donated gold and silver ritual utensils. In 1983 the King of Nepal donated an eight metal alloy *ashtadhatu* bell.

The gateway to the main courtyard has finely wrought brass doors and above the gate is the *naubat khana* where *shehnai* players perform every dawn to wake Lord Vishwanath and usher in a new day. The courtyard is surrounded by small shrines dedicated to many deities and worshippers do *puja* at all of them before heading for the sanctum sanctorum, the *garbha griha* where Vishwanath, the Lord of the World waits for his devotees.

The doors to the *garbha griha* are made of silver and exquisitely engraved. The *lingam* of Vishwanath is made of black stone and is set in a silver lined square recessed altar set into the floor. There are five main *arti* ceremonies and before each the deity is decorated by the presiding priests. Chanting Vedic *shlokas* they bathe the *lingam* in honey, ghee, milk, *bhang* and *gangajal*, then the three stripes of the *tripundraka* mark are drawn on it with sandalwood paste and vermillion. Then covered with marigolds, roses, jasmine and Shiva's personal favourites – garlands of hibiscus flowers and bilva leaves. Lord Vishwanath disappears under his decorations and the silver coils of a cobra curve around the lingam with the open hood of the snake flaring above it.

This *lingam* is a *swayambhu* that manifests itself and is not a creation of people. As the greatest of Kashi's *lingams*, Vishwanath – Vishweshwara is often linked with the greatest of the river ghats, Manikarnika and the two of them are said to constitute the axis of Kashi's religious life. As the sixteenth century poet Narayan Bhatta writes, "One who bathes in Manikarnika bathes in all *tirthas*. One who sees Vishweshwar makes all pilgrimages. One should always see Vishweshwar and always bathe in Manikarnika. It is true, true, over and over."

There are five daily *artis* conducted by eleven priests to the blowing of conches, the beat of drums and cymbals. The chanting of *mantras* is interspersed by calls of 'Har Har Mahadev!' and 'Jai Bholenath!' from the watching throng as the smoky, incense filled air throbs to prayers and praises. The

TEMPLES OF VARANASI 83

tall brass lamps glittering with flames light up Lord Vishwanath as the *mantras* and music reach their crescendo.

There are five *artis* at the temple. The first Mangala arti to wake the deity is at 3.30 am. The second, Bhog arti, when Lord Vishwanath is offered the *naivedyam* food is at 12 noon. The Saptarishi arti welcomes dusk at 7.30 pm. The Shringara arti, when Lord Vishwanath is specially decorated in a long ritual of shringara is at 9.30 pm and the final arti before the god's repose, the Shayan arti is at 10.30pm. The temple closes at 11 pm. Only on the night of Shivaratri it stays open till the next dawn.

Right before the doorway of the sanctum sits a giant Nandi bull of marble. Among the shrines in the courtyard dedicated to various deities is the ancient *lingam* of Avimukteshwara that is said to be older than Vishwanath. Most of the ancient treatises mention it and it was worshipped during the time of the Guptas. Today it only has a small corner of the temple. The goddess shrines are of Virupaksha Gauri, Saubhagya Gauri, Shringara Gauri and Savitri. There are many other *lingams* like Nikumbheshwara, Kapileshwara, Mahakala, Nilkantheshwara, Kubereshwara, and Vaikuntheshwara. The Ganesh shrines include Vighneshwara Ganesh and Avimukta Vinayaka that once stood in the old Avimukteshwara temple.

There is also a shrine to Vishnu in the main mandapa of the temple and this deity is always worshipped along with Vishwanath. Devotees performing the *nitya yatra*—the daily pilgrimage, begin at Kashi Vishwanath and then visit the Gyan Vapi well and the temples nearby of Annapurna Bhavani, Dandapani and Dhundiraja Ganesh.

The Gyan Vapi well

The well of wisdom, stands under an open arcaded pavilion that was built in 1828 by Baija Bai, the wife of Gwalior's Daulat Rao Sindhia. The well is said to have been dug by Shiva himself with his trident and the water is used to bathe the *lingam* of Vishwanath. As the name suggests, its waters are said to be a liquid form of enlightening wisdom. Pilgrims sip the water from this well before going for *puja* into the temple.

About the myth of the Gyan Vapi the *Kashi Khanda* writes, "Isana, the Rudra, finding the place congenial took up his famous trident and dug with it a great pond, and then with its waters bathed the universe in its *linga* form. Thousand upon thousand of jars of water were used for bathing the *lingam*. This pleased Rudra and he desired to bless the place. He announced that the word Siva (wherein all find rest) in fact means Sublime Realisation. The state of attainment of this realisation has been materialised in the form of water with which this great tank has been filled. Hence this pond with its water shall be known as Jnana-da or Jnana-vapi."

The Gyan Vapi mosque was built using the fragments of the Adi Vishweshwara temple and patches of beautiful carvings, pillars and lintels can still be seen embedded in its walls and doorways. One wall of the Adi Vishweshwara temple covered in ornate carvings still stands, as do beautiful columns that now flank one of the doors of the mosque. The proximity of the temple and the mosque has for centuries made this space volatile with religious passions that continue to bubble under the surface even today.

Sakshi Vinayaka Temple

In this temple Ganesha as Sakshi Vinayaka performs a very important function. He is a *sakshi*, a witness and his job is to maintain a record of the pilgrims who visit the Kashi Vishwanath temple or perform the various *yatras*. Pilgrims come here so that benign Vinayaka, the celestial record keeper can bear witness to their merits gained. This small shrine stands near the Kashi Vishwanath temple and was built by the Marathas in the eighteenth century.

Kashi is supposed to have fifty six shrines dedicated to the elephant-headed Ganesha as the remover of obstacles and giver of boons. In the Divodasa myth when all the gods had failed to restore Kashi to Shiva it was clever Ganesha who devised the way to make Divodasa leave the city. Shiva was so pleased that he gave the name of Dhundiraja to Ganesha. There is a small shrine to Dhundhiraja in the Vishwanath gali and it is said to be the centre of the divine *mandala* of Kashi within which all the deities reside. Among the other important Ganesha shrines are Arka Vinayaka near Asi ghat, Durga Vinayaka next to the Durga temple, Kharva Vinayaka near the Adi Keshava temple and Siddhi Vinayaka near Manikarnika ghat.

Bare Ganesha Temple

This is the most popular Ganesha shrine in the city. As Bare or 'Big' Ganesha he is called Maharaja Vinayaka in the *Puranas*. The spacious temple stands in the Saptasagara area of the city. The most important festival at this temple is of Ganesh Chaturthi when the temple is crowded with devotees.

Annapurna Bhavani Temple

There are many goddess temples in Kashi including Durga, Vishalakshi, Shitala and Sankata Devi, however the pre-eminent goddess of the city is Annapurna Bhavani. As Shiva's consort she is the queen of Kashi and presides over the *tirtha* and sits beside him. Luminous and benign Annapurna is the generous goddess of plenty and as Bhavani she is Shiva's *shakti* and his manifest source of power. The *Kashi Rahasya* says, "For happiness there is no home like Kashi; there is no father like Vishweshwara and there is no mother like Bhavani, destroyer of rebirth; and there is no household like the people of Kashi, who are Vishnu incarnate!"

Annapurna is the true Mother Goddess, generously providing food and good crops to her devotees. The myth of the temple says that Shiva requested that Annapurna should feed all the people of Kashi. When she became worried at the difficult task, Ganga assured her that for every spoon of food that she served, the river would provide a pot of water.

Unlike most of the other goddesses like Durga and Kali who have both dark and luminous aspects, Annapurna is all benign. So she does not carry any weapons and usually holds the pot of plenty and a ladle to give the food. She sustains life, nourishes her devotees and promises abundance in life. She and Shiva make the perfect divine couple as she sustains life and Shiva provides *moksha* after death. As many of the folk paintings of Annapurna show, even Shiva as the wandering *sadhu* comes to her and begs for food.

The Annapurna Bhavani temple stands in the Vishwanath Gali very near the Kashi Vishwanath temple and pilgrims all head for it after their *puja* of Shiva. The original temple was also destroyed during medieval times and this shrine was built in 1725 by the Maratha ruler Peshwa Baji Rao I. The temple courtyard fills with devotees during the nine days of the Navaratra in spring and autumn. The silver image of Annapurna in the sanctum is a new one and was installed by the Shankaracharya of Shringeri in 1977. There is an older image of Annapurna made of solid gold that is opened for *darshana* only during the three days of the great Annakuta festival every autumn.

Annakuta or the mountain of food, is a harvest festival celebrated during the *shukla paksha* of Kartik just before Diwali. The temple porch is covered in a veritable mountain of cereals, lentils, fruits, vegetables and an endless variety of sweets and this is distributed as *prasada* to the devotees. On that day Lord Vishwanatha is also in a generous mood and *prasada* is distributed at his temple. Another Annapurna puja is celebrated in the month of Magh for the rice harvest and the goddess and her temple are decorated with green sprouts of paddy.

Durga Temple

This is a popular temple dedicated to the warrior goddess and is famous for its large tank called Durga Kund. Durga is believed to be the protector of Kashi. Unlike most of the temples in the heart of the city that are housed in cramped lanes, the Durga temple stands within a spacious courtyard and with the stepped Durga Kund beside it. The present temple was built in the eighteenth century by Rani Bhawani, the queen of Natore, a small principality in Bengal. It was designed in the classical northern *nagara* style of architecture and painted a distinct terracotta colour.

The temple stands on a high platform set within a quadrangle court. Carved images of lions, Durga's mount, sit before the entrance. It has twelve carved pillars that support the many tiered *shikharas*. There is a *naubat khana*, a music gallery above the entrance gateway where musicians still play at dawn and dusk. The *natya mandapa*, a music and dance pavilion is attached to the main shrine.

The myth of the temple as related in the *Kashi Khanda* tells the tale of the classical battle of the goddess with the demon named Durg. This demon had become invincible through his years of asceticism and no god could defeat him. Even Indra, the king of the gods was forced to leave his throne because of Durg. Finally the gods came to Shiva and begged that only the Devi could vanquish him. So the Devi and her cohort of fighting goddesses went out to battle. In a mighty battle that shook the earth Durg kept changing his form from an elephant to a charging bull. The Devi finally pierced his heart with her trident and killed him. The battle is said to have taken place where the Asi ghat now stands. After the battle a tired Devi rested by the Durga Kund and dropped her giant sword, an asi, and it cut a channel into the earth along which the Asi river began to flow. The Devi, as the slayer of Durg now took the name of Durga.

The image of Durga in the sanctum is a wide eyed silver mask. Devotees come especially on Tuesdays and Saturdays to do puja. In the month of Shravana a mela takes place around the shrine. Many people simply call this the monkey

The New Vishwanath Temple built by Pandit Madan Mohan Malaviya. (inset) The 18th century Kashi Vishwanath Temple.

The sacred ghat of Manikarnika, where a goddess lost her earring.

Sunrise over the Ganga river.

A morning massage on the ghat.

Flower sellers in the Kashi Vishwanath Gali.

(top) Evening arti on Dasashwamedh Ghat.
Diyas floated on the river by pilgrims.

(top) The famous Banarasi silk saree.
A weaver at work on his loom.

(top) The Kedareshwar Temple on top of Kedar Ghat.
(centre) Sadhus meditate by the river.
The Durga Temple and Durga Kund.

(top) Puja lamps at a brass shop.
(above) A delicious display of ladoos at a sweet shop.

Preparations for a puja on a ghat.

(top) Idol of Bhairon, a companion of Lord Shiva.
(centre) The Charanapaduka Temple on Manikarnika Ghat.
(above) Image of Lord Buddha at Sarnath.

A panorama of the eighty ghats of Varanasi.
(below) The temple that sank into the river at Dasashwamedh Ghat.

Great citizens of Varanasi.
(top) The 16th century poet Tulsidas, composer of the Ramcharitmanas.
(left) The 15th century Bhakti poet Kabir.
(below) Ustad Bismillah Khan, the shehnai maestro.

temple because of the hoards of troublesome monkeys that wander around the courtyard.

An interesting story connected to this temple tells of a British Collector of Banaras, William James Grant who in 1808 presented the temple with one of the bells hanging in the porch. It is said that one day when he and his family were crossing the Ganga his boat was caught in a whirlpool and the boatman managed to save them after praying to Durga.

Vishalakshi Temple

This ancient temple to the goddess Vishalakshi stands in a narrow lane behind Mir ghat. It is one of the few Kashi temples that is mentioned in a twelfth century compendium of shrines by Lakshmidhara that lists the various Devi *pithas*, the seats of the goddess. The *pithas* are the fifty two places where parts of the body of Sati landed after she killed herself. At this *pitha* they say the eyes of Sati fell and according to Tantrik beliefs her shrine is guarded by Kal Bhairava who is a fearsome aspect of Shiva. As Vishalakshi, the Devi is the 'wide eyed' goddess. The Devi is also worshipped as Meenakshi, the 'fish eyed' goddess at Madurai and as Kamakshi, the 'love eyed' goddess at Kanchipuram and in Assam. Like the Kedareshwar temple, the shrine dedicated to Vishalakshi is extremely popular with the South Indian community.

Kal Bhairav Temple

In Hindu mythology a *bhairav* is the fearsome aspect of Shiva. When Shiva is in a rage then he allows the bhairavs to emanate from his body and wreck vengeance on his enemies. There are supposed to be sixty four *bhairavas*, the same number as *yoginis*, who are an aspect of the Devi. A *bhairav* while merely an aspect of Shiva is also worshipped as a separate deity. The *bhairavs* who are also called *bhairons* follow Shiva as his loyal companions or *ganas* and their altars are often connected to Shiva shrines. A *bhairav* is a terrible demi god with fang-like teeth, a moustache, wearing a garland of skulls and he carries a club. He rides a dog and his club is called Dandapani. In Kashi, Kal Bhairav, the black *bhairav* is called the *kotwal* or police chief of the city. Dandapani who is also worshipped separately is his sheriff.

The temple of Kal Bhairav, also called Bhaironath by the local people was built by Peshwa Baji Rao II in 1825 and is located between Chaukhamba Lane and Maidagin. The gates of the temple are guarded by carved figures of dogs and the small shrine stands in the middle of a courtyard. The only part of the image in the sanctum that is visible is the face of the deity and it is a gleaming silver mask. In the myth of the *jyotirlingam* when Shiva was angered by Brahma, Kal Bhairav appeared and cut off Brahma's fifth head. The skull stuck to his hand and Kal Bhairav wandered around all the *tirthas* of the land in penance and it is only when he reached Kashi that the skull fell away. During his wanderings from one *tirtha* to another Kal Bhairav used the skull as a begging bowl. The esoteric *tantrik* sadhu sect of *kapaliks* or 'skull bearers' worship Bhairav and carry skulls like him. Devotees try to please a Bhairon with offerings of liquor and candy dogs.

Shiva appointed Kal Bhairav as the superintendent of justice in his city and so they say, "In Kashi, Vishwanath is the king, Annapurna the queen and Kal Bhairav the governor". Kal Bhairav devours all the sins that are left behind in Kashi by pilgrims. He also keeps a record of the deeds of the people of Kashi, so devotees worship him to keep this relentless and unforgiving deity happy. Finally he also passes judgement on the karma of those who have died in Kashi, judging both their good and bad deeds. When anyone dies in Varanasi they are made to face the "bhairav yatna" – suffering the pains of hell for their sins for a moment, before they reach heaven. Kashi also has temples to two other *bhairavs* – Lat Bhairav and Dandpani.

Sankat Mochan Temple

This ancient temple standing in a picturesque setting among trees is located near Asi ghat, on the road to Banaras Hindu University. It is said to have been established by the poet Tulsidas. Dedicated to Hanuman it is one of the most popular temples among the citizens of Varanasi who believe in the power of the benign monkey god in delivering them from their problems. The temple is the site of many religious discourses, music festivals and *melas* held during the year in its sylvan surroundings.

Tilbhandeshwar Temple

This rather spartan temple stands off Madanpura Road and houses one of the largest Shivalingas in the city. The giant column is said to grow by the height of a *til*, a sesame seed, every day and that gives the temple its strange name. The *linga* is over a metre tall and is also very broad. The temple is patronised more by the locals than by pilgrims. On Shivaratri night the *linga* is decorated with flowers, *bilva* leaf garlands and then a five headed copper mask is placed on top of the column. The faces show Shiva with raised eyebrows and curling moustaches!

Tulsi Manas Temple

This twentieth century temple is one of the most beautiful shrines in Varanasi. Built in gleaming white marble in the traditional nagara style with many-tiered *shikharas* and spacious *mandapas*, this shrine was really created in worship of the saint Tulsidas (1552-1623). In the sixteenth century this great bhakti poet wrote the immortal epic *Ramcharitmanas,* in which he retold the story of the *Ramayana*. What made it unique was that he wrote it in the local language instead of Sanskrit. This made this great book accessible to ordinary people and gradually it became a deeply venerated text. Today all across north India people read the *Ramcharitmanas* like the Bible and it brings them great solace.

The Tulsi Manas temple set within landscaped gardens was built in 1964 and the walls are inscribed with all the verses of the *Ramcharitmanas* and painted with murals showing scenes from the epic. The sanctum has icons of Rama, Sita, Laxman, Hanuman and also an image of Tulsidas. The temple museum also has a collection of rare *Ramayanas* written in many languages of the world.

Kabir Temple

Another poet saint is worshipped at this shrine that stands in Kabirchaura, the locality where Kabir stayed. No one knows whether Kabir (1398-1448) was a Muslim or a Hindu. He was abandoned by his mother and brought up by a poor weaver couple Neeru and Neema. Kabir was accepted as a disciple by Swami Ramananda after he lay down in his path on Panchganga ghat. One of the greatest poets of the medieval age his short pithy verses called *dohas*, have now become a part of language of the people. Kabir opposed the injustice of caste, the worship of idols and religious bigotry. He sang the praises of the one common formless god who only needed to be worshipped through *bhakti*, a passionate love that needed no priests, no holy books or special *mantras*.

All his life Kabir continued to work as a weaver and many of his verses are woven around the imagery of looms, cloth and threads. His wise, observant words were often aimed at the bottomless superstitions of the pilgrims coming to Kashi expecting miracles from the priests and he sang,

> "Going on endless pilgrimages
> The world died,
> Exhausted by so much bathing."

The sect worshipping Kabir are called Kabir panthis and this simple sandstone temple is built where his dilapidated hut once stood. Here all they worship are Kabir's portrait, his wooden clogs, his rosary and a bowl, all lovingly preserved in the sanctum. In the serene, welcoming ambience of the temple the verses of Kabir's *Bijak* are sung as prayers all day.

The temple blends Hindu and Islamic architectural styles and is the centre of religious discourses. People also come here to meditate in special meditation chambers. Even after seven centuries Kabir's enlightened spirit lives in this serene shrine dedicated to a great philosopher and poet who spoke in the voice of the simple and poor folk of Kashi.

Even today when the world is divided by endless religious conflict, Kabir's wise words as translated by Rabindranath Tagore stay significant and relevant,

> "If God be within the mosque, then to whom does this world belong?
> If Ram be within the image which you find upon your pilgrimage,
> Then who is there to know what happens without?
> Hari is in the East; Allah is in the West.
> Look within your heart, for there you will find Both Karim and Ram."

New Vishwanath Temple

This is another modern temple and was built in 1966 inside the campus of the Banaras Hindu University by its founder Madan Mohan Malaviya. Once the Kashi Vishwanath temple was opened to people of all castes there was a huge outcry from superstitious orthodox brahmins. They decided to build a new temple called Adi Vishwanath. The New Vishwanath temple was Malaviya's response to this act of caste prejudice. Here everyone of every caste, creed and nationality is welcome.

Funded by the Birlas the exquisitely designed marble temple stands in the midst of beautiful landscaped gardens and shady trees. It is built in the architectural design of the Adi Vishweshwar temple of Raja Todar Mal that was destroyed by Aurangzeb. There are two *garbha grihas* in the double story temple, one with a *lingam* and the other with a carved image of Shiva as the divine ascetic. The *sandhya arti* at this temple, with the metronomic beat of giant drums and the clashing of huge cymbals echoing across the shrine is worth attending.

The Bharat Mata Temple

This is a truly unique temple dedicated to Bharat Mata, or India as a goddess. The shrine therefore has no idols, bells or carvings, only has a giant map of India! The detailed relief map is engraved on a slab of marble and the purpose was to foster patriotism among people. It was built by a nationalist leader, Shiv Prasad Gupta, and Durga Prasad Khatri, a leading antiquarian and numismatist of Varanasi, and formally opened by Mahatma Gandhi in 1936.

There are some rather strange temples in this city of shrines. In the Vishwanath Gali there are three temples that worship planets: the Shanichar temple dedicated to Saturn, the planet that is supposed to bring bad luck, the Shukreshwar temple is dedicated to the planet Venus where women pray for sons, the Brihaspati temple is devoted to Jupiter and young boys and girls pray here for good spouses. The Briddhakal temple is supposed to help in the curing of the diseases of old age. Shitala is the goddess of small pox and her temple stands on Dasashwamedha ghat where people pray to her to cure skin diseases.

The goddess called Achanak Devi is depicted as a metal mask and is said to relieve people of restlessness of the mind. The goddess of the city, Varanasi Devi has a tiny shrine near the Panchganga ghat. The Dandapani temple actually worships Kal Bhairav's great stone club which is named Dandapani and which he uses against sinners. Nearby is a well called Kal Kup, or the Well of Fate. The Kashi Karawat temple has the *lingam* placed inside a dry well and a huge rusty axe, a *karawat*, is placed beside it. Legends say that at one time devotees wanting a short cut to heaven used to chop off their heads with it. Nowadays the sensible priests do not allow people to climb down into the well and all that the devotees can do is drop small pieces of lighted camphor as offering.

Festivals of Kashi

They say there is a festival every day in Kashi. There are enough temples, ghats, gods, goddesses, *yoginis*, *yakshas* and *bhairavas* to make that possible. There are the usual festivals of the Hindu calendar like Holi and Diwali and also those special to a temple or a ghat and some festivals that are unique to the city. Also there are seasonal fairs, the joyous melas that spring up along the lanes filled with makeshift open air stalls selling toys and trinkets, pottery, woodcrafts, clothes and food. The dates of many festivals change from year to year as they are according to the Hindu lunar calendar. Here we are listing the festivals that are unique to Kashi or celebrated in a special way.

January to March

Makar Sankranti, is usually the first festival of the year, when people bathe in the Ganga on a freezing January morning. Then special food of a rice and lentil *khichri* and the *til laddu*, a sweet made from sesame seeds are prepared for lunch. In the evening people crowd the roofs flying kites.

Basant Panchami is a spring festival when everyone wears festive yellow clothes. They worship Saraswati, the goddess of learning with yellow flowers, especially the first blossoms of the mango tree.

Shivaratri is the most important festival in Kashi. It is the Great Night of Shiva, celebrated on a moonless *amavasya* night in the month of Phalgun. People fast all day and stay awake all night singing hymns in his praise. Every Shiva temple and shrine is filled with devotees and the *lingams* and images covered in flowers. The most gorgeous celebrations are in the Kashi Vishwanath temple where the lane is jammed with people as they celebrate the marriage of Shiva and Parvati. A magnificent wedding procession called Shiva Baraat meanders through the lanes jammed with people. It is also said to be the night when Shiva, as Nataraja, the Lord of the Dance dances the magnificent *tandava*.

Rangbhari Ekadashi is a special day when Lord Vishwanath is decorated in a very elaborate *shringara* ceremony. The shivalingam is covered with flowers, hibiscus garlands, *bilva* leaves and sandalwood paste. Then a silver four faced mask is placed on it and instead of *gangajal* and milk, devotees consecrate the deity by spraying it with vermilion powder.

Holi is the festival of colours celebrated all across the land. In Kashi *holika* fires are lit the night before to drive out evil and the next day the city sways to a bacchanalia of colour, intoxicants, music and dance. Shiva's favourite intoxicant of *bhang* and *ganja* are mixed into *thandai* drinks and a variety of savouries and sweets. At Chaumsatthi ghat there is a fair to honour the *chaunsath yoginis*, sixty four female divinities who are the companions of the Devi..

April-June

Ganga Saptami & Ganga Dashahara are two festivals that worship the Ganga's arrival on earth. On Ganga Saptami the celestial river began her descent from heaven and on Ganga Dashahara she entered the plains. Dasashwamedha ghat is crowded with bathers and people go out in boats and trail miles of marigold garlands across the waters in a loving worship of their Mother Ganga.

July-September

Chaturmasa is the four monsoon months when *sadhus* move into spiritual retreat and often stay at the many *ashrams* in the city. Here people gather to listen to discourses and recitations from the holy books.

Lolarka Shashthi is celebrated at the pool called Lolarka kund, near Asi ghat. Childless couple offer flowers and vegetables in this ancient shrine to Surya praying for children.

October-December

Pitripaksha is the fortnight in Kartik that is dedicated to the worship of ancestors is of great significance in Kashi. Pilgrims arrive to perform *shraddha*, funeral rites and *tarpana* to worship ancestors and pray for their peace.

Navaratra and Dussehra are the nine days celebrating the Devi. The Bengali community celebrates the Durga Puja, building exquisite earthen images of the warrior goddess killing the demon Mahishasura. The first Durga Puja celebrated outside Bengal was at Varanasi in 1773. On Dussehra as the Durga images are immersed in the Ganga, in other parts of the city effigies of Ravana, Kumbhakarna and Meghnad explode in a shower of fireworks.

Ram Leela is the folk drama based on the *Ramayana*. Navaratra is also the time the famous *Ram Leelas* of Kashi enact the eternal epic of the *Ramayana*. It is said the first *Ram Leela* was performed here by Tulsidas on Asi ghat. The oldest Ram Leela of the city, called Adi Ram Leela is performed at Lat Bhairav and this has scenes that are a series of pageants and have no dialogues. The pageant of Ram Bharat Milap is held at Nati Imli and Nakkataiya at Chetgunj and thousands gather to watch them. The most famous is the *Ram Leela* at Ramnagar patronised by the Maharaja of Kashi. It is based on the *Ramcharitmanas* and the episodes are enacted at different locations in a series of sets. People gather every day to watch the actors enact the battle of Ram and Ravana, some in elaborate make up and the others wearing bright papier mache masks.

Deepavali is the *amavasya* night in Kartik when Ayodhya welcomes a triumphant Rama by lighting earthen lamps. The finest show of this festival of lights is at the ghats that glow to hundreds of lamps turning them into a fairyland of black and gold. Houses glitter with lights as Lakshmi, the goddess of prosperity is welcomed into every home.

Annakuta is celebrated in the Annapurna Bhavani temple where huge piles of cereals, lentils, fruits, vegetables and sweets are offered to the goddess and then given away to the people.

Kartik Purnima has the ghats once again glowing with lights as lamps float in the river. The best celebration is on Panchganga ghat where the *akash deeps,* the sky lamps, are placed in bamboo baskets hung on top of poles to light the way for the dead throughout the month of Kartik. A tall pillar, the *Deepajhara sthambha* with a thousand wicks is lit and its glow is visible like a fiery beacon of benediction across the waters.

Nag Nathiya celebrated at Tusi ghat is part of the enactment of the *Krishna Leela,* the life of Krishna. The scene of Krishna killing the serpent Kaliya in the episode of the *Kaliya Daman* is enacted here.

A Lunar Calendar of pujas in Kashi

- Chaitra (March/April)—Navaratra, Ram Navami, Holi.
- Vaishakha (April/May)—Akshaya Tritiya, Trilochana Darshana, decoration of Manikarnika Kund, Ganga Saptami.
- Jyeshtha (May/June)—Shitala ashtami, Ganga Dashahara.
- Ashadh (June/July)—Shitala ashtami, Rath Yatra, Vishnu Shayani Ekadashi.
- Shravana (July/August)—Nava Gauri, Naga Panchami.
- Bhadrapada (August/September)—Kajali Tij, Ganesh Chaturthi, Janamashtami, Haritalika Tij, Lolarka Shashthi.
- Ashvina (September/October)—Pitri Paksha, Navaratra, Durga Puja, Vijaya Dashami.
- Kartik (October/November)—Dhanteras, Hanuman Jayanti, Deepavali, Annakuta, Bhima Dwitiya, Prabhodini, Vaikunth Chaturdashi, Kartik Purnima.
- Agrahayana (November/December)—Bhairava Ashtami
- Pausha (December/January)—Paush Purnima, Makar Sankranti
- Magha (January/February)—Mauni Amavasya, Vasant Panchami
- Phalguna (February/March)—Maha Shivaratri, Rangbhari Ekadashi.

Six

HISTORY OF VARANASI
Ancient and Still Eternal

*"Oh well born of Banaras, I too am born well known.
My labour is with leather
But my heart can boast the Lord."*

—Ravidas, Fifteenth century Bhakti poet

HISTORY OF VARANASI

If the earth and river at Varanasi could speak they would have an unforgettable tale to tell us. Varanasi has seen more than any other city in the world. As the oldest living city in the world it has witnessed every age of Indian civilization. From the arrival of the ancient Aryans, the conflicts of the kings of the Mahabharata to the invasions of Ajatshatru, the royal generosity of the Mauryan king Ashoka, the bigotry of Aurangzeb to the ambitions of Warren Hastings, Varanasi has seen them all.

Here all the great deities of Hinduism have taken form in iconography and their mythology, worship and rituals have been crystallised until they became the great religious movement that we call Hinduism. Kabir and Tulsidas have sung their songs beside the Ganga here and Patanjali and Ramanuja have spread their knowledge and wisdom among the people. The greatest thinkers and teachers of their times, Gautama Buddha, Vardhaman Mahavira, Adi Shankaracharya and Guru Nanak have come to this centre of learning to listen and debate, preach and guide people. For centuries it has remained at the centre of India's spiritual soul.

Kashi-Varanasi finds mention in innumerable ancient texts in all the major Indian languages. In Sanskrit we find it in the *Rig Veda*, *Satapatha Brahmana*, *Brihadaranyaka Upanishad*, *Aitereya Brahmana*, *Manusmiriti*, *Chandogya Purana* and the *Arthashastra* of Kautilya. As also in the writings of travellers like Megasthenes in the third century BC, Huien Tsang in the seventh century AD and Al Biruni in the twelfth century AD. With them there are the books of praise, called *Mahatmayas* written on the city like the *Kashi Khanda*, the *Kashi Rahasya*.

Kashi as Shiva's Forest of Bliss, still symbolises knowledge and wisdom for the Hindu. For thousands of years it has welcomed seekers of truth—scholars, sadhus and students. It is where the great wealth of Hindu scholarship is still preserved. In the mind of the Hindu "Going to Kashi" means not just a pilgrimage but also heading to the fountainhead of wisdom. Kashi is never far from the mind of Hindus as a lifelong aspiration. In some weddings there is an amusing ritual when the groom threatens to retire to Kashi as a scholar to study the Vedas and then has to be persuaded to remain with gifts and compliments. The ritual of the sacred thread ceremony, the *upanayana*, includes the young initiate taking seven symbolic steps towards Kashi.

Unlike other cities Varanasi is oddly indifferent to its history. It gathers stories instead—intricate myths about its deities, legends of long forgotten kings and folk tales of hunters and boatmen. They write books of praise about the many myths of Shiva and his favourite city, the memories of poets whose songs they sing and about miracles of faith. Few have bothered to chronicle the events of the past in an organised manner.

Scholars speculate about the name Kashi. Was it the name of the Aryan tribe that settled here or of the kingdom? The *Puranas* mention a King Kasa of the Pururavas dynasty whose grandson was Dhanvantri and the legendary King Divodasa, who threw Shiva out of the city, was Dhanvantri's grandson. One of the earliest references to the city, in ancient texts is in the *Mahabharata*, where a king of Kashi is often mentioned. The king's three daughters – Amba, Ambika and Ambalika were abducted by Bhishma to be married to Vichitravirya. Later a Kashi king took part in the great battle of Kurukshetra.

By the sixth century BC a number of powerful Aryan kingdoms had emerged in the Indo-Gangetic region called *janapadas* and among them the three most powerful ones were Kashi, Koshala to its north and Magadha to its east. The history and royal genealogies of these three powerful kingdoms, which were often at war, has been chronicled in both Hindu and Buddhist texts, like the *Puranas* and the Buddhist *Jataka* tales.

The names Kashi and Varanasi can be found often in the Jataka tales that narrate the lives of many mythical Buddhas or bodhisattvas who appeared before Gautama Buddha. According to them the kingdom was called Kashi and its capital was the magnificent city of "Baranasi". The city measured twelve leagues and was surrounded by a high wall and is admiringly described as "the chief city of India" and one tale says, "all the kings round coveted the kingdom of Baranasi". When the Koshala king conquered Kashi he took the proud title of 'Baranasiggaho', conqueror of Varanasi. The Buddhist text *Mahavagga*, written in the sixth century BC refers to it as a Mahajanapada, a great city. It describes Varanasi as *surandhan*—safe, and *sudarshan*—pleasant. It also calls the city Kasinagar and Kasipur and mentions the fabulous wealth of the merchants of the city called *shreshtis*.

Varanasi in the time of the Buddha was a prosperous centre of commerce. Some of the *Jataka* stories begin with the phrase "once a rich merchant of Baranasi", and in one story a future bodhisattva is a rich *shreshti* who was doing business with five hundred carts of goods. It was a natural site for commercial activity as it stood beside the Ganga that has always been used extensively for trade. Also the Northern Road connecting the east and north to the western ports swept past the city. So Varanasi prospered as a trade and handicraft centre and even at the time of the Buddha its weavers were famous for the fineness of their cotton textiles.

After the Buddha had preached his first sermon at Sarnath to five bhikshus, his first lay disciple was Yasa, the son of a rich *shreshti* of Varanasi and it is with this conversion that Buddhism took its first step towards becoming a popular religion. It is said that after the Buddha's death the shroud was presented by the weavers of Varanasi and it was woven so fine that the cloth did not even absorb oil.

The history of Varanasi begins in the Rajghat Plateau. It is the high area at the northernmost end of present day Varanasi, right near the Malaviya Bridge that spans the Ganga and the Adi Keshava ghat. As archaeological excavations have shown, this grassy plateau standing between the Ganga and Varuna rivers, is the area with the oldest settlement in Varanasi. Today as the city has moved southwards, except for the Adi Keshav temple, this region has turned into a rural enclave of the city.

As the Buddhist texts tell us, in the sixth century BC, Kashi became embroiled in a battle for supremacy between Magadha and Koshala. First King Prasenajit of Koshala conquered Kashi. Then when he wed his sister Chellana to Bimbisara, the powerful Magadhan king, he gave Kashi as the dowry for the queen's, "expenses for bathing and perfumes". Both Bimbisara and Prasenajit were devotees of the Buddha. Before he arrived in Varanasi, the Buddha had converted Bimbisara. When he met the Buddha, Prasenajit was so impressed by him that he married a Sakya princess.

Bimbisara was later killed by his son Ajatshatru and Queen Chellana, mother of Ajatshatru, is said to have died of grief.

Angry at the death of his sister and her husband, Prasenajit then attacked and defeated Ajatshatru and retrieved Kashi. However an alliance with Magadha was obviously of great value because he then married his daughter Vajira to Ajatshatru and again offered Kashi as dowry. Ultimately Magadha became the supreme power in the Indo-Gangetic region and both Kashi and Koshala became a part of Ajatshatru's kingdom. Kashi would remain a part of the kingdom of Magadha even in the time of Ashoka who came to visit Sarnath.

However there are no archaeological remains to substantiate the written histories of Kashi, Koshala and Magadha. The earliest dated remains are the pottery, artefacts and section of a city wall excavated in the Rajghat plateau dated to the third century BC. Coins of Lalitaditya, the king of Kashmir found here prove he had entered Kashi in the eighth century AD. The Palas, Pratiharas, Rashtrakutas, Chandelas and Chedis at some time or other held Kashi. The Rajghat area must have been inhabited for a long time as it was still the main settlement during the reign of the Gahadavala kings in the twelfth century just before the arrival of the Muslims. There are inscriptions in the Adi Keshava temple recording donations by the royal family and of their taking a dip in the Ganga there.

The last Gahadavala king was the infamous Jaichand who refused to help Prithviraj Chauhan against the armies of Muhammad Ghori as Prithviraja had eloped with his daughter Sanyukta. Later the Ghori armies would defeat and kill Jaichand and the rule of Hindu kings over Kashi would come to an end. Then in the 1190's Ghori's general Qutubuddin Aibak invaded Kashi and destroyed the city, looting the temples and flattening the palaces. The settlement moved southwards and the Rajghat area was never inhabited again.

From the time of Ajatshatru to the arrival of Qutubuddin, Kashi was a commercial centre and it was even more significantly the intellectual heart of the land. From Rajghat a high ridge runs southwards parallel to the Ganga, where the three hills that are symbolic of three prongs of Shiva's trident stand. This forested ridge was watered by small streams that ran into the Ganga, though most of them have dried out by now. Along these streams and especially at the point of their confluence with the Ganga stood the hermitages of the *rishis*—sages and scholars who welcomed students to their peaceful forest retreats. Gradually as the city moved southwards these *ashrams* vanished. The top of the ridge was then taken over by the city and the steps of the ghat were built to run down from it to the river.

Shravasti, the capital of Koshala, Rajagriha and later Pataliputra, the capitals of Magadha were centres of political power but Kashi was the true centre of learning. After being absorbed into the kingdom of Magadha, politically Kashi became less significant but continued to thrive for its intellectual activities. At these *ashrams* of the *rishis* some of the greatest scholarly writings were produced not just on religion and philosophy but also astronomy, grammar, medicine and mathematics. In spite of it being a holy city, Kashi was also an egalitarian and free thinking university of ancient India. It encouraged a freedom of thought that is in sharp contrast to its present day image as a centre of orthodox, blindly ritualistic Brahminical beliefs.

What was worshipped in Kashi was *gyana* – knowledge, not caste or religion. A great guru or *rishi* was respected for the depth of his knowledge, not his caste. For instance many of the *Upanishads* were written here and their authors were not brahmins and they often questioned prevalent religious and philosophical practices. As Abraham Eraly writes in his book *Jewel in the Lotus*, "The *Upanishads* mark a radical transformation in the religion of Aryans, by shifting its emphasis from gods and rituals to abstract concepts and mystic knowledge. This did not, however, involve any cultural discontinuity."

The authors of the *Upanishads* were discovering a new path for the study of the *Vedas*, a more questioning way that ignored rituals and challenged the Brahmin's claims of monopoly of all knowledge. Most of the *Upanishads* were composed between the seventh and fifth century BC and their authors preferred philosophical and mystical questioning to ritual sacrifices as described in the *Vedas* and *practised* by the brahmin priesthood. The *Upanishads* speak of looking for a god within and search for a sacred force called *Brahman*. The way to gain *moksha* is through an inward transformation not the performing of external rituals. As the Mundaka Upanishad says so lyrically,

> "Take up thy bow, the *Upanishad*, a mighty weapon.
> Fit in thine arrow sharpened by devotion,
> Stretch it on thought allied with resolution—
> This is the target friend,
> The Imperishable. Pierce it!"

North India seemed to have teemed with such spiritual seekers and both the Buddha and Mahavira were a part of the same stream. Like the Buddha, many of these great thinkers were in fact *kshatriyas*, who were seeking answers to the eternal questions of existence, creation and death as they were reluctant to take refuge in blind, unquestioning rituals. They were looking for wisdom and enlightenment through *gyana*, or knowledge that could lead to *moksha*.

Even kings became involved in such philosophical quests. It is said that King Ajatshatru was so knowledgeable that he taught some of the brahmins in his court. Another legend is about Balaki, a brahmin who was very proud of his learning. He offered to teach the king of Kashi the meaning of life. As a test the king asked him to explain the nature of the *Brahman*. Balaki showed him the Vedic symbols of the divine like the sun, moon and lightning but the king was not satisfied. Finally the king spoke of the *atman* and the practising of yoga to gain *moksha* and enlightened Balaki.

Many schools of thought emerged from the ashrams of Kashi. Among them the most influential were the schools of Sankhya, Yoga, Mimamsa, Vedanta, Nyaya and Vaisheshika. These classical schools would continue to inspire thinkers into the modern age, including Adi Shankaracharya and Swami Vivekananda. Among the thinkers who worked in these *ashrams* were great scholars like the grammarian Patanjali, in the second century BC, Shankaracharya in the eighth century and Ramanuja in the eleventh century AD, followed by great teachers like Madhavacharya, Vallabhacharya and Ramananda who all established monasteries here. There are also *mathas* here of every major Hindu sect like the Gorakhnathis, Aghoris, Vira Shaivas, Kabir panthis and the followers of Ma Anandamoyee.

One of the earliest sages to come to Varanasi was Siddhartha Gautama, the Buddha, when he came from Gaya

HISTORY OF VARANASI   111

after his enlightenment and met many of the philosophers here. Then he walked to the outskirts to a park called Rishipatana, a place where many ascetics stayed and there he gave his first sermon, called the *Dharma chakra pravartana*, the turning of the wheel. Today we know Rishipatana as Sarnath that was later covered with stupas and viharas by Ashoka and other kings.

Siddhartha was a prince of the Sakya clan of Kapilavastu who had wandered in the Magadhan kingdom of Bimbisara and gained enlightenment there. So there was no reason for him to come to Varanasi except that it was the centre of learning and the best place to test his new philosophy. As historian Moti Chandra explains, "Varanasi at this time was so celebrated that it was only suitable for the Buddha to teach a new way and turn the wheel of the law here." Later the Buddha spent many of the monsoon retreats at Rishipatana. Like Varanasi, the flourishing monasteries of Sarnath also fell prey to the rampaging armies of Qutubuddin in the twelfth century. Varanasi managed to rise again but as its ruins still show, Sarnath never recovered.

In the same way the *tirthankaras* of the Jain faith also came to Varanasi. The seventh *tirthankara* Suparshva was born here and so was the twenty third *tirthankara*, Parshvanatha who lived here in the eighth century BC. The great Vardhaman Mahavira, who was a contemporary of the Buddha visited Varanasi. So Varanasi is also a Jain *tirtha* as the Jain ghat shows. In the fourteenth century the Jain scholar Prabha Suri listing Jain *tirthas* mentions Varanasi which had a temple to Parshvanatha. Today there is a shrine dedicated to Parshvanath in the locality of Bhelupura.

Through the ancient period Varanasi continued to flourish as the centre of learning for the Hindu sects of Shaiva, Vaishnava, Shakta and of the Buddhist and Jains. If Ashoka came to Sarnath and built a stupa, Pushyamitra Sunga came to perform an *ashvamedha yagna* in Varanasi. Temples were built during the Gupta period and then in the seventh century, during the reign of Harsha of Kanauj, the Chinese bhikshu Hiuen Tsang visited Varanasi on his way to Sarnath. His writings describe a picturesque city surrounded by clusters of villages, with temples set in sylvan settings, shaded by trees and standing beside flowing streams. The city had streets lined by the houses of wealthy people and the people were highly civilized and educated.

With the rule of the Gahadvalas in the eleventh century Kashi once again became the political centre of a kingdom. The Gahadvalas ruled for over a century with their capital at Kanauj but also gave prominence to Kashi as a religious and administrative centre. They were Vaishnavas and the Adi Keshava temple has inscriptions recording their patronage. In mid twelfth century, during the reign of Govindchandra his chief minister was the scholar Lakshmidhara who compiled a *nibandha* called *Krityakalpataru*. This was a compendium of quotations from ancient texts and it had a section on the *tirthas* of the time called *Tirthavivechana Kanda*. The largest section is devoted to Varanasi and he lists 350 shrines in the city.

The last Gahadvala king Jayachandra continued his feud with the Chauhan king of Delhi, Prithviraja, and when the armies of Muhammad Ghori invaded he refused to help. Prithviraja died on the battlefield in 1192 and Jayachandra met the same fate two years later. Ghori's general Qutubuddin

Aibak then entered Varanasi and sacked the city. The Muslim historians claim that one thousand temples were razed to the ground and mosques built in their place. After the pillage, a train of 1400 camels carried away the plunder. Varanasi's dark days had begun.

Through the years of the Delhi Sultanate and then the Mughals, Varanasi got little respite from the plunder of kings. The only time when the *tirtha* was allowed to draw a breath of liberation was during the reign of Akbar, when the tolerant Mughal emperor allowed the temples of the city to be built again. Raja Man Singh built the legendary Bindu Madhav temple and the ghats of Mansarovar and Man Mandir. Raja Todar Mal patronised the building of the Adi Vishweshwarya temple. Akbar had appointed Todar Mal's son Goverdhan as the governor of Varanasi at that time and is said to have visited the city and Sarnath. His royal historian Abul Fazl refers to Varanasi as the premier of the seven holy places, writing, "From time immemorial, it has been the chief seat of learning in Hindustan. Crowds of people flock to it from distant parts for purpose of instruction, to which they apply themselves with the most devoted assiduity."

Another Mughal who looked kindly on Varanasi was Shahjahan's philosopher son Dara Shikoh who was the subedar of the province. Dara employed Kashmiri pandits who had settled in Varanasi to translate the Upanishads into Persian and the volume was titled *Sir-i-Akbar*. However in the battle for the throne Dara lost to Aurangzeb and Varanasi also paid the price.

A list of raids between the twelfth and eighteenth centuries says it all. Kashi has lost track of the times it was demolished. Every time the people would abandon the rubble and move further south to build again, a tenacious courage that seemed to enrage the Muslim kings. Razia Sultan's armies came after Qutubuddin, followed by Firuz Shah Tughlak. Then the city fell into the hands of the Sharqi nawabs who carted away the walls of the temples to build mosques in their capital Jaunpur. The Lal Darwaza mosque was built with the fragments of the Padmeshwara temple. Then Sikander Lodi came in the sixteenth century. After the benevolence of Akbar, his son Jahangir left Kashi alone and his grandson Shahjahan did not attack the established temples but all the shrines that were under construction were demolished. Then Shahjahan's son Aurangzeb's armies swept into Varanasi with a zealot's passion and wiped out Kashi once again.

The whole medieval period is a time of destruction, revival and destruction once again. If Bindu Madhav, Omkareshwar, Krittivas, Adi Vishweshwara, Kal Bhairav, Mahadeva, Madhyameshwara are all just names carried in the collective memory of the city it is because Aurangzeb wiped them out of existence. He replaced Bindu Madhav with the Alamgir mosque and Adi Vishweshwara with Gyan Vapi and then renamed the city as Muhammadabad, even issuing coins stamped with it. However he died soon after and the people forgot the new name with alacrity. Some of the deities were saved and hidden in small houses like Bindu Madhav and Kal Bhairav, the Vishweshwara lingam probably lay submerged in the Gyan Vapi well only to be enshrined in new temples in the eighteenth century. However some like Krittivasa and Madhyameshwara vanished forever. The only structures from Akbar's time that survived were the two ghats built by Raja Man Singh.

The spirit of the city showed in the tradition of scholarship and philosophy that continued through the upheavals of the medieval period. Much of the *Puranas* were compiled at this time. The *Kashi Khanda*, the book of praise of the city was completed and also other such *mahatmyas* like the *Kashi Rahasya* and the *Kashi Kedara Mahatmya*. Narayan Bhatta who gained Todar Mal's help to rebuild Adi Vishweshwara also compiled *Tristhalisetu* with verses in praise of the three *tirthas* of Kashi, Prayaga and Gaya. In Shahjahan's reign Jagannatha composed his paean to the River Ganga, *Ganga Lahari*, that the people of Kashi still sing in praise of the river.

This was also the time of the evolution of the Bhakti movement. It was a popular mystical faith inspired by an intense devotion to one god that produced some of the finest poetry of the medieval times. Just as there were the Alvar and Nayanmar saints in the south singing the praises of Vishnu or Shiva, the mystic poets of Varanasi too became a part of this resurgence. Bhakti, a passionate and very personal form of worship did not need the intervention of brahmins, it eschewed rituals and many of the teachers welcomed disciples from every caste. One of them in the fifteenth century was Swami Ramananda among whose followers was a barber, an untouchable, a woman and a weaver.

This weaver was Kabir, one of the finest poets of the time. His short, sharply observant verses have now become a part of the language. No one knew if Kabir was a Hindu or a Muslim as he addressed his god as both Ram and Rahim. He was a follower of a Muslim pir and of Swami Ramananda. He ridiculed both the mullah and the brahmin asking people to seek their god within themselves through love and devotion.

Just as he showed his disdain of people going on pilgrimage to Mecca or to Kashi. As he wrote,

> "I have seen the pious Hindus, rule followers,
> Early morning bath takers, killing souls.
> They worship rocks.
> They know nothing.
> I've seen plenty of Muslim teachers, holy men
> Reading their holy books,
> And teaching their pupils techniques.
> They know just as much."

Sixteenth century saw the appearance of another great bhakti poet, Tulsidas. He was fortunate to live in Kashi during the reign of Akbar and so worked during a time of peace and renaissance. He even wrote in praise of the new Bindu Madhav temple. A devotee of Ram and Hanuman he recreated the *Ramayana* in the vernacular, Avadhi. The Sanskrit text of the epic had been the monopoly of brahmins but now with Tulsidas' *Ramcharitmanas* the *Ramayana* became accessible to the people. Since then it has become the favourite religious text of the Hindi-speaking world with devotees reading and reciting its verses every day.

After the decline of the Mughals, the Marathas played a very constructive role in the life of the city. Kashi had once given shelter to Chhatrapati Shivaji when he escaped from the imprisonment of Aurangzeb. Now the Maratha royalty patronised a revival of the *tirtha* after the powerful Mahadaji Sindhia got the right to rebuild Varanasi from the Mughal king Shah Alam. In present day Varanasi, most of its ghats and many of the temples are a gift of the Maratha royal families like the Peshwas, Holkars and Sindhias. Among the important shrines built by them are Trilochana, Annapurna, Sakshi Vinayaka and Kal Bhairava. The most prominent of course being the Kashi Vishwanath temple built by Rani Ahalyabai Holkar of Indore. In the eighteenth century the Maratha chieftain Sadashiv Rao Peshwa came to live in Kashi, bringing a thousand brahmin scholars with him and they did much to revive Sanskrit scholarship here.

Varanasi finally returned to the rule of a Hindu king during the eighteenth century. During the reign of Muhammad Shah, the subedar Mir Rustam Ali handed over the city to a local brahmin landowner Pandit Mansaram and his family continued to rule through the British Raj days. Even today the Kashiraj has an important role to play in the religious life of the city and also as patron of the art and culture of Varanasi. One of the kings of this dynasty was the famous Chet Singh who, in 1781, refused to pay revenue to the British, forcing the governor general Warren Hastings to come to Varanasi to confront him. Chet Singh who was imprisoned in his palace on Shivala Ghat, managed to escape and lead a rebellion forcing Hastings to flee from Varanasi, though ultimately the kings had to accept the suzerainty of the British.

During the years of the freedom struggle the Indian National Congress held its session of 1904 in Varanasi. The city's scholastic traditions have continued even into the modern age. The British had established the Sanskrit College here in 1791. Then Pandit Madan Mohan Malaviya worked tirelessly to establish the Banaras Hindu University that was established here in 1916 on land that was donated by the Kashiraj. The

Kashi Vidyapeeth was established in 1921. Annie Besant and J. Krishnamuthy also established schools here. Then in 1947, when India attained independence, the kingdom of Kashi was absorbed in the Union of India.

Seven

VARANASI TODAY
Mauj and Masti Among the Cows

"Benaras is older than history, older than tradition, older even than legend, and looks twice as old as all of them put together!
—Mark Twain, *Following the Equator*, 1896.

There is a warning that the people of Varanasi give to the unwary pilgrims wandering like lost sheep along its narrow streets, "beware of four things in Kashi—widows, bulls, ghat stairs and holy men", and the warning is often followed by a wide grin revealing paan stained teeth. There are other things one should be prepared for in ancient and cynical Kashi—hordes of beggars, aggressive pandas looking for customers to fleece, and ambling cows. Also goats chewing marigold garlands they have purloined off a deity somewhere, monkeys waiting to ambush pilgrims at temples for the prasad and some of the loudest and most persistent vendors in the land. Not to forget rickshaw pullers, boatmen, *bhang* makers, street singers, Ganga water and flower sellers and men who will sidle up to you in dark corners and offer you anything you want. Today's Varanasi has this ability to simultaneously enchant and repel, amuse and anger but it never leaves a visitor untouched.

The people of this city, the famous Banarasi, have this aggressive, cynical, slightly rustic, at times deliberately crude style oddly at variance with the venerable history of the *tirtha* they live in. They describe the typical Banarasi attitude to life as *mauj*—a festive mood, *masti*—joie de vivre and *phakkarpan*—a carefree humour. This mauj and masti that the people enjoy comes with a rough edge because being a citizen of Varanasi is not an easy act of survival. They have their own schools of classical music and dance, provide a home to scholars and teachers and they also grind *bhang* on the ghat steps, sit at *paan* shops and sing ribald songs at passing women and treat pilgrims as easy picking for their confidence tricks. Kashi never flinches from revealing its myriad faces to the world.

To discover the world of the Banarasi you have to venture into its labyrinth of lanes, the famous *Kashi ki gali*, those narrow, dark serpentine passages with high, teetering houses on both sides where the local people live. These densely populated *galis* join to form localities called *mohallas*. The heart of the city is these *mohallas* that form an impenetrable maze called the *Pukka Mahal*, tightly packed with people and teeming with perpetual movement. The *Pukka Mahal* is still stuck somewhere in the medieval ages and changes come very slowly and imperceptibly here. Huge joint families, comprising many generations live here in crowded houses so old and badly maintained they are often on the edge of collapse. Many can trace their history back for centuries in a misty mix of memories and family legends.

Walking down a *gali* is quite an experience. They are so narrow that at places there is space for just one person to pass and one has to flatten oneself against a wall to let rickshaws and vendor's carts go by. The houses on both sides are often so high little sunlight penetrates the gloom and the sky is just a flash of blue past the sagging balconies and mesh of crisscrossing electric wires. The walls of the houses are often painted with brightly coloured folk paintings of deities and you walk along in their divine and benign company. Shiva blessing you at one doorway, Ganga riding her strange dolphin like beast and smiling by a verandah. In an ancient and cosmopolitan city, these paintings add a surprisingly homely, earthy touch to the ambience.

As you are wandering along a *gali* you may encounter one of the famed bulls of Banaras as it comes swaying towards you and you have to do some quick acrobatics by jumping on to a verandah or sliding into a corner to avoid them. Within these constricted spaces there are temples and shops, workshops, restaurants and Internet cafes. Also pigeons cooing on the parapets, monkeys swinging along the cornices and a solemn sadhu sitting in a niche in the wall. As you pass by look closely at the arch of a stone doorway or a drooping balcony and you'll discover some exquisite medieval carvings under the layers of grime and bright paint.

The mohallas are alive with movement throughout the day and late into the night. Many lead to the ghat, so at dawn when the temple bells ring out pilgrims and local devotees hurry from their early morning dip in the Ganga to catch the first *arti* of the day. Little girls in school uniform, their hair tied in bright ribbon bows go chattering by, as the vegetable vendor's call echoes along the lane. Going past the *mithai* shop you catch a whiff of boiling milk and a flavour of saffron and at the teashop the hot glasses of *chai* warm up the loud arguments about cricket or politics. In the lanes where the weavers work, every inch of the balcony walls is covered with the many hued skeins of silk thread drying in the sun—brightening the air with their jewelled hues of crimson and aquamarine, gold and emerald. The world of the *mohallas* is a very special space—the people may not be rich but they have the security of close knit traditions of many generations of living together and the sense of being a true community.

Over the centuries many of these *mohallas* have gathered people of different regions. There is the Bengali Tola along the lanes near Kedar Ghat, Jains around Jains ghat, the Sindhis and Gujaratis live in Soniya, the Punjabis in Lahori Tola, South Indians in Chaukhamba, Afghans in Benia Bagh and local Muslims are concentrated in Madanpura and Jalalipura. Some localities are named after famous people like Daranagar after Dara Shikoh, Kabir Chauraha after the Bhakti poet, Nawabganj after Nawab Saadat Ali of Avadh, Govindpura after Raja Govindchandra of Kanauj. While Lahurabir and Bhojubir were tribal heroes whose legends may have been forgotten but their names still survive on the addresses of letters.

The best known *gali* of all is of course the Vishwanath Gali that is a legend all across the land. This lane leading to the Kashi Vishwanath temple is never still. It is lined with shops, temples, restaurants and ancient guest houses. It is in fact a maze of lanes with the shops selling everything from sarees, garish artificial jewellery, attar perfumes, second hand books, musical instruments, *ayurvedic* medicines and all the brass, wood and silver paraphernalia needed for *puja*. As you near the temple gates the flower shops begin with the shopkeepers filling the air with their raucous welcome, sitting behind mounds of golden marigolds, hibiscus garlands, *bilva* leaves and fragrant roses.

Another colourful gali is Thatheri Bazaar that takes off from the Chowk. Pilgrims all head here because anything you need in a temple, your *puja* room or for any special religious ceremony can be found here. There are brass and copper utensils, images of deities, lamps and holy garments for the idols bright with tinsel. Satti Bazaar is the world of the silk saree. In fact there are a number of such bazaars in Golghar, Lukkhi Chabutra, Kunj Gali and Ranikuan where the weavers bring their creations that are auctioned by saree dealers, the *gadidars*. The weavers arrive carrying the dazzling silks covered in gold and silver work in long cardboard boxes and then begin the complex negotiations with the *gadidars* in a mystical code of numbers.

The *akharas* are another unique aspect of *mohalla* life. These traditional gymnasiums have aspiring wrestlers hard at work under the guidance of their gurus. Lifting wooden weights, swinging huge clubs, hanging from ropes or scrabbling around on the soft earth of the wrestling arenas. As the system of yoga is a combination of physical and spiritual well being, some of the hermitages also have their *akharas* like the Niranjani, Nirvani and Juna Naga *akharas*, where the ascetics work hard on physical fitness. During medieval times these naga sadhus fought pitched battles with the Muslim armies in vain attempts to protect the temples. One of the fiercest was against Aurangzeb to save the Adi Vishweshwara shrine. On early morning boat rides some of these muscle bound men, their bodies glistening with oil can be seen at their exercises or getting massaged on Hanuman ghat and many of the star wrestlers and body builders become local heroes.

If the stages of a Hindu's life, the *purushartha* include the four phases of *dharma – artha – kama – moksha*, Varanasi offers all of them. It is the *tirtha* where people come seeking a good death and it has always been a city of the good life. So if you have Manikarnika and the hostels where people come to die, you also have great wealth, music, dance, paintings and good food. Even in the time of the Buddha, Kashi epitomised luxury and the finest things of life. Once while talking of how gently he was nurtured by his father King Shuddhodhana, Gautama Buddha said,

"Monks, I was delicately nurtured, exceedingly delicately nurtured, delicately nurtured beyond measure... No sandalwood did I use that was not from Kasi; of Kasi cloth was my turban made; of Kasi cloth was made my jacket, my tunic, my cloak. By night and day a white canopy was held over me, lest cold or heat dust or chaff or dew touch me."

Merchants have come to Kashi because great fortunes could be made here through trade and selling to pilgrims. Cotton textiles and later also silk woven in Kashi were treasured in ancient Rome for their fine weaves. The merchants called Kashi 'jitvari', a city of victory as you could win great wealth doing business. In a *Jataka* tale one merchant is described as having goods filling five hundred carts and the Buddha's first lay disciple Yasa was a merchant prince of the city. The *Jataka* tales often mention the 'rich merchants of Baranasi' and also the courtesans at its temples.

Originally chosen to perform for the deities in the temples, these courtesans also played a part in the city developing its own schools of classical music and dance. The art of the Kathak dance and musical styles like *thumri* can be traced to the art of the *devadasis* who performed in the temples. In the medieval times the courtesans of Kashi were famous not just for their performing arts but also their cultured ways. Every evening the upper crust Banarasi would put on a crisp *dhoti kurta*, dab on fragrant *attar*, wrap a *mogra* string around his wrist, pop a *paan* into his mouth and venture out to visit his favourite courtesan. To listen to the plaintive strains of the *thumri* and *kajri* and to the jangle of anklets appreciate the dazzling footwork of *Kathak*.

Varanasi's tradition of performing arts has continued into present times. In music the classical forms of *dhrupad*, *dhamar* and *khayal* are combined with light classical styles like *thumri*, *kajri* and *chaiti*. The folk songs can still be heard sung by women during festivals as they go in procession to the river bank. The Banaras *gharana* has produced celebrated musicians like Omkarnath Thakur, Bismillah Khan and his incomparable shehnai and *thumri* singers like Siddheshwari Devi, Rasoolan Bai and Girija Devi. The classical dance of *kathak* is still taught here and famous dancers have included Sitara Devi and Gopi Krishna.

For a true Banarasi, an important part of the *masti* of life is of course good food followed by the perfect *bida* of *paan*. Varanasi has a Kachauri Gali and a Khowa Gali and when people name *galis* after a kind of fried bread and a milk concentrate you know they take their cuisine very seriously. For the Banarasis take pride in being connoisseurs of the right *kachauri*, the perfect *mithai* and the precisely made *paan*. Kashi's food shops offer examples of the best of the vegetarian cuisine of Uttar Pradesh and also samples of the cuisine of the communities settled here like the sweets of Bengal.

Kachauri Gali runs parallel to Vishwanath Gali and hungry pilgrims head for it seeking a meal after their early morning fasts. At the *kachauri* shops the cooks sit before huge *karhais* of smoking hot oil frying the crisp and crunchy *puris*, *kachauris* and *pakoras*. The *kachauris* are fried pastry with a lentil stuffing served with an *aloo bhaji*, spicy potatoes and pickles. Puris, plain fried wheat breads go best with chick pea *ghughni* with a subtle gravy. The *pakoras* are chunks of seasonal vegetables dipped in a gram flour batter and deep fried to a golden crisp. Or you may try the triangular *samosas*, flour pastries stuffed with potatoes. For snacks gram flour is used in many inspired ways to make *papad*, *chura*, *bhujia* and *dalmoth*.

Then those looking for dessert, the *mithai* shops have shelves of sweets in a delicious and indulgent menu. You get the twists of *jalebis* still dripping with hot syrup or may be a glass of cool creamy *lassi*. The sweet platter includes the local speciality the *peda* and thick sweetened milk called *rabri* that is served in earthen bowls. There are laddus, *malpua*, *khaja*, *balushai*, *mohan bhog*, *malai gujiya* and a variety of *barfis*. Also the Bengali sweets made of cottage cheese like milky white balls of *rosogollas*, *chamcham* and *sandesh*. The gods obviously love these sweets as they are offered daily at the temples. In the hot summer months the most popular drinks are *lassi* and *thandai*. The smoothly frothy *lassi*, made in a creamy blend of milk and curd flavoured with saffron is drunk from earthen cups. The *thandai* comes in a variety of recipes, some are made of milk, topped with dried fruits and saffron and can be spiked with intoxicating *bhang*, especially during the festival of Holi. After a foray into a *mithai* shop you realise that Kashi brings you many kinds of *moksha* after all!

Two food items are named after the city – the banarasi *langra*, one of the best mangoes of north India and the banarasi *paan*. They sing songs about *paan* and it is a symbol of not just romance but also friendship and celebration. Once courtesans reddened their lips with the spiced rolls of betel leaf, the *bidas* of paan covered in silver foil. *Paan* is still offered to guests and business negotiations are traditionally sealed by an exchange of *bidas*. *Paan* is offered to the gods as part of *naivedyam*, and every Banarasi prides himself at being a connoisseur of the heart shaped betel leaf. They even have a market for *paan* where the leaf coming from various parts of the country and baskets of *maghai*, *kapoori* and *mahoba paan* are auctioned. Every lane has its *paanwalla*, sitting perched behind the brass bowls of lime and catechu paste, *zarda* tobacco, rose jelly called *gulukand*, camphor, cardamom and coconut powder and baskets of fresh betel leaves.

One form of handicrafts bears the name of the city—the banarasi saree. Since ancient times the silks and cottons from the looms of Varanasi have travelled to many corners of the globe. The weaving industry began here first to supply cotton and silk to the temples and now it is Varanasi's biggest handicrafts. As Macaulay describing Kashi in the eighteenth century as a centre of the textile trade wrote,

> "Commerce had as many pilgrims as religion. All along the shores of the venerable stream lay great fleets of vessels laden with rich merchandise. From the looms of Benaras went forth the most delicate silks that adorned the balls of St. James's and of Versailles; and in the bazaars, the muslins of Bengal and the sabres of Oude were mingled with the jewels of Golconda and the shawls of Cashmere."

In the shops you can see yards of shimmering silk covered in a dazzling array of motifs—flowers and vines, dancing peacocks and paisleys. The silks of Kashi were legendary and every Hindu bride has at least one Banarasi silk in her trousseau. It was called *kassiya* or *kashivastra* and wandering down the lanes of Alaipura, Lallapura and Madanpura where the weavers stay, you can hear the clack of the looms and see the multihued skeins of silk and cotton drying in the sun. The *kinkhab* was made for royalty and was so stiff with gold thread it was used for the formal robes worn at the durbar. The richest silks woven today are the *jamdani* brocades woven with gold and silver *zari* threads. And there is the delicate, pastel shaded *tanchoi*, with an embossed weave that is said to have come from China. The *baluchari* originally came from Bengal with human figures woven into the *pallav*. In Varanasi they brighten it with *zari*. The *valkalam* uses only silk threads to recreate the motifs from Mughal miniatures. The weavers of Kashi proudly claim that you only have to show them a weave and a motif and they can produce an exact replica on their magical looms.

The creations of the craftsmen and folk artists of Kashi can be found at the *melas* that spring up all through the year. The potters bring their wares in August-September to the Sorahaiya ka mela dedicated to them. Using the clay from the banks of the Ganga the potters create bowls, pots, vases and rustic toys. The wooden toys and images of deities are brightly painted and the woodcarver also makes the utensils for the *puja* room. Kashi's folk artists still paint miniatures in their typical, vibrant styles and they are the folk painters are the ones decorating the walls of the houses along the *galis*. The crafts in brass, copper, papier mache and jewellery can be found in the shops in the main bazaars and *galis* of Varanasi.

Varanasi is still an important centre of traditional learning like yoga, ayurveda and astrology, *jyotishcharya*. Lord Shiva is also mahayogi, the Lord of the Yogis as he meditates in the mountain heights of Kailash. So Shiva's city is naturally a centre of the science and philosophy of yoga. Shiva is said to have founded the system of yoga and his consort Parvati was his first disciple. As enunciated in the *Upanishads*, achieving a pure consciousness is central to the Shaivite philosophy and of yoga. Many of the *Upanishads* were composed in Kashi, so it has been a centre of yoga from the beginning. This ancient science blends *asana*, *dhyana* and *pranayam*—physical exercises and postures, meditation and exercises in breath control and is aimed at achieving *moksha*. In many of the *ashrams* and *mathas* around Varanasi yoga is taught to students trying to achieve a discipline of the mind and the body, through asceticism and meditation to gain a serenity of spirit.

Ayurveda, 'the knowledge of long life' is the traditional Indian system of medicine and healing. Ayurveda is an ancient system of balancing the various energies of the body with the outside environment to gain better health. The system has been explained in the two treatises *Charaka Samhita* and the *Susruta Samhita*, compiling the knowledge of two great physicians—Susruta and Charaka. Susruta is said to have founded the Varanasi school of Ayurveda. The ayurvedic shops, many in Vishwanath Gali sell herbal cures and ayurvedic doctors give advice on proper dietary habits, the use of lifestyle changes and ways to achieve spiritual well being.

Just like the *paan* shops, you can find an astrologer in every *gali* and *mohalla* of Varanasi. For people believing in the stars and the effect on their lives of their cosmic movement, astrology is a living tradition and thriving business in Varanasi. The astrologers of the city have been famous for centuries and even today the *Panchang*, the Hindu calendar and almanac is compiled here. The *Panchang* gives the dates of festivals, *pujas* and also makes predictions and suggestions to gain benefits and avoid disasters.

Jyotishcharya, the Indian system of astrology is based on both the lunar and solar calendars. Kashi *jyotishis* use astrological charts marking the position of stars, numerology and palmistry to make their predictions and they are patronised not just by ordinary people but also political leaders and big industrialists. The astrologers are everywhere—in large houses, in temples, by the ghats and perched beside their brightly coloured boards by the road. They prepare charts for weddings, study them to predict the future, before any major decision being taken in business or politics and offer *rudraksha* beads, talismans, charms, amulets and gemstones to ward off evil. A few minutes listening to their starry sales talk by the side of a road can be an amusing way to end a walk along a Kashi *gali*.

Eight

SARNATH
Buddham Sharanam Gatchami

"I shall go to Banaras where I will light the lamp that will bring light unto the world. I will go to Banaras and beat the drums that will awaken mankind. I shall go to Banaras and there I shall teach the Law"

—Gautama Buddha in Bodh Gaya.

Two thousand years ago a prince who had become a wandering ascetic came to the banks of the Ganga at Varanasi with a message of enlightenment. As the saffron clad monk wandered along the lanes of the city of Kashi, listening to the teachings of brahmins and sages or entered the shadowy groves of the hermitages that surrounded the city, few would have given him a second glance. After all, this was a time of great religious ferment and philosophical questioning and there were many like him wandering around Kashi in their search for answers to eternal questions.

Siddhartha Gautama, the Buddha had gained enlightenment by the banks of the Nairanjana river and then walked from Gaya, crossed the Ganga by ferry to reach the ghats of Kashi. He left Kashi and went to the sacred grove of Rishipattana where his friends, five ascetics were meditating. In a discourse to them he unveiled the wisdom he had gained after his experience in Bodh Gaya. This first sermon is called *Dharmachakra Pravartana*, the turning of the wheel. Unfolding his path of enlightenment, Gautama Buddha spoke of the Four Noble Truths and the eightfold path or the 'middle way'. The Truths were about 'dukkha', suffering, the causes of suffering, the cessation of suffering and the way to achieve that through the middle way. This way was the eightfold path of right views, aspirations, speech, conduct, living, effort, mindfulness and meditation. The five ascetics then became his first disciples.

Rishipattana is today known as Sarnath and if Varanasi is Shiva's city, this is Gautama Buddha's retreat. The ambience of these two places seems to reflect the contrasting natures of their two presiding deities. After the frenetic volatility of

Varanasi, peaceful Sarnath welcomes you with a gentle, serene smile. It is just ten kilometres away from Varanasi, so after discovering the magic of the ghats and the temples take a short drive to the quiet, welcoming emerald groves of the Buddha's Sarnath.

The presence of the Great Teacher still permeates the hoary ruins of stupas looming over the expanse of lawns and the walls of ancient monasteries covered in creepers. He walks beside you in companionable silence down the path to the red roofed *vihara*. He is there to listen to your half spoken prayers by the spreading branches of the Bodhi tree under which the deer wander. Stand by the doorway and listen to the deep droning chant of the monks interspersed by the clang of bells. Then stroll across the lawns where at dawn the dew lies shimmering like spangled stars and the grass is strewn with windblown flowers. The monks from the *viharas*, in their ochre robes go by chanting softly. If you are looking for peace and a few moments of reviving solitude, spend some time at beautiful Sarnath.

The place was called Rihsipattana because sages, the *rishis* and ascetics, the *sadhus*, came here to meditate. As it was a deer park it was also called Mrigadaya, the deer sanctuary of the king. The name Sarnath is probably a simplified version of the name of a Bodhisattva called Saranganatha, the Lord of the Deer. Here Gautama Buddha also found his first lay disciple in Yasa, a merchant prince of Kashi who came from the city and begged to join the Buddha. With the induction of Yasa, his family and friends as his disciples the Buddha began the Sangha, the Buddhist monastic order.

For the next forty five years the Buddha would wander the kingdoms of Magadha and Kosala in the Indo-Gangetic plains on a peripatetic mission of preaching but he did not forget Sarnath. It was one of his favourite monsoon retreats when during the *chaturmasa*, the four months of the rains, he stayed in the monastery here and spent time in solitary meditation. So Sarnath like Lumbini, where he was born, Bodh Gaya, where he gained enlightenment and Kushinagar, where he gained *nirvana*, became the four most important places of pilgrimage after his death, places to be visited with "reverence and awe". Then when Buddhism gained royal patronage during the reign of Ashoka and then the Kushans, Sarnath became a centre of the religion, with *viharas* teeming with monks, *stupas* and *chaityas* being added by rich patrons. Sarnath remained a great centre of Buddhism for a millenium and a half, right till the twelfth century.

In the fourth century BC the greatest royal patron of Buddhism, Emperor Ashoka, the Mauryan king of the kingdom of Magadha came from his capital Pataliputra to Sarnath and built the *stupa* here over the relics of the Buddha. Later he added other *stupas*, the monasteries, the *viharas* and prayer halls, the *chaityas* and erected pillars. During the reign of the Guptas in the fifth century AD the Chinese pilgrim Fa Hien visited Sarnath and in his writings mentions two monasteries and two *stupas*. Hiuen Tsang came here in the seventh century AD and mentions a large establishment of many monasteries and 1500 monks at prayer in the *vihara* temple. Also *stupas*, Ashokan pillars, lakes and gardens. In the twelfth century Kumaradevi, the Buddhist queen of King Govindachandra of Kanauj repaired some of the *viharas* and also built a new *vihara* and many gateways.

The most detailed description of ancient Sarnath can be found in the travelogue of Hiuen Tsang. He writes, "to the north-east of the Varana we come to the Sangharam of Luye (Deer Park). Its precincts are divided into eight portions connected by a surrounding wall. The storeyed towers with projecting eaves and the balconies are of very superior work. There are 1500 priests in this convent who study the Little Vehicle according to the Sammitiya School. In the great enclosure is a *Vihara* about 200 feet high. Above the roof is a gold covered figure of the *Amra* or mango fruit. The foundations of the building and the stairs are of stone, but the niches are of brick arranged in a hundred successive lines and in each niche is a golden figure of the Buddha. In the middle of the *Vihara* is a figure of the Buddha made of native copper (brass). It is the size of life and he is represented as turning the Wheel of Law."

With the arrival of the Muslims, Sarnath like Varanasi suffered greatly at the hands of the invaders. During the invasion of Qutubuddin Aibak in 1194 the monasteries were pillaged and burnt, the few monks who survived fled. Then through the medieval period even though Varanasi would rise again and again, Sarnath would lie in ruins forever. Buddhism was already in decline by the twelfth century and it would vanish from India in the following centuries and Sarnath would be forgotten by the people.

It was discovered again in 1834 when a British archaeological team led by Sir Alexander Cunningham began excavations here. The *stupas* were unearthed and with the discoveries in Sanchi and Bodh Gaya, the Buddha appeared once again in the history and heritage of the country. As

Cunningham wrote, "I found about sixty statues and bas reliefs in an upright position, all packed closely together within a small space of less than ten feet square." For 1500 years Sarnath was a prosperous centre of Buddhism and excavations done here have led to the discovery of many ancient artefacts. The most famous is the remnant of the Ashokan pillar and its lion capital that is today the symbol of the Indian government.

The ruined Dhamekh Stupa and Dharmarajika Stupa are the two most significant remains of ancient Sarnath. The latter was probably built at the site where the Buddha gave his first sermon. Scholars speculate that the original *stupa* may have been built by Ashoka and had contained relics of the Buddha. Later additions were made during the Gupta and Kushan periods. Some broken pillars and railings show that the *stupa* was probably surrounded by a carved stone railing and gateways like the *stupa* at Sanchi. It is in a very ruined state because in the eighteenth century Jagat Singh, the Dewan of Varanasi, had much of it demolished, its bricks were carted off and used to build a bazaar in the city. During this wanton destruction a marble casket was discovered that later reached the Asiatic Society in Calcutta.

The Dhamekh Stupa was probably built in the sixth century AD during the reign of the Guptas and was built over an older Ashokan *stupa*. The name Dhamekh is probably derived from the Sanskrit *dharmeksha*, meaning the "pondering of the Law". The Dhamekh Stupa is not the egg-like shape of the traditional *stupa*, but a more cylindrical structure. The tower rises to a height of 33 metres and at the base it has a diameter of 28 metres. The lower portion is made of stone and the upper of dressed brickwork that has a carved stone facing. The base is broken by niches where images of the Buddha were placed and is carved with an elegant and intricate border of floral and geometrical patterns.

There may also be the remains of another *stupa* on the road from Varanasi to Sarnath. The high grassy mound is called Chaukhandi and it is topped by a medieval octagonal pavilion. Buddhist traditions say that this *stupa* was built during the Gupta period to mark the site where the Buddha first met his five companions. The octagonal pavilion on top was built in the sixteenth century by Goverdhan, the governor of Varanasi. He was the son of Raja Todar Mal and built it to celebrate a visit by Akbar to Varanasi and Sarnath.

Hiuen Tsang describes a shrine at the site where the Buddha used to meditate when he stayed at Sarnath during the monsoon retreats. The shrine was called Mulagandhakuti. A statue excavated here shows a Bodhisattva and the inscription on it says that it was installed by Bhikshu Bala of Mathura in the first century and it also mentions the name of the shrine. In the twentieth century Anagariha Dharmapala, the founder of the Mahabodhi Society of India began the work of preserving the remains in Sarnath. He first purchased the land and in 1922 laid the foundation of a temple here that he named Mulagandhakuti Vihara in memory of the ancient shrine.

The new *vihara* is an elegant structure built in the traditional style with an arched roof and a large prayer hall. It is placed within a picturesque garden and inside it are enshrined relics of the Buddha which were discovered in Taxila, Nagarjunakonda and Mirpur Khas in Sind. The walls of the prayer hall are covered in frescoes painted in the Ajanta style by the Japanese artist Kosetsu Nosu and depict the various important episodes from the life of the Buddha. Outside the Mulagandhakuti Vihara there are emerald lawns where the deer wander under the shady branches of a Bodhi tree that grew from a sapling that was brought from Anuradhapura in Sri Lanka. The Bodhi tree at Anuradhapura had grown from a sapling from the original tree at Bodh Gaya that was sent by Ashoka to Lanka.

The Sarnath Museum and sculpture shed are a treasure trove of Buddhist artefacts—sculptures, bas relief, ancient manuscripts, carved panels, pillars, railing fragments, terracotta figurines and pottery ranging from the Mauryan, Gupta, Kushan periods and the reign of the Gahadvalas. There is the most famous of the Ashokan capitals that once crowned a pillar whose stump still stands near the Dhamekh Stupa. It is topped by four roaring lions facing the cardinal directions and symbolises the spread of *Dharma* across the world. Below is an inverted lotus and animal figures interspersed by the sacred wheel. Once the lions were topped by another wheel, a *dharmachakra*, the wheel of law, whose fragments were discovered beside the pillar.

The museum has some exquisitely carved images of the Buddha. Many were carved during the Gupta period using the sandstone from nearby Chunar. There is a standing image with sensitively carved flowing robes and the inscription says it was donated by the monk Bala in the third year of the reign of the Kushan king Kanishka. Once this standing figure was shaded by a stone umbrella that is displayed nearby. The image of the preaching Buddha shows him seated, his hands in the preaching posture and with a halo behind him. This sculpture is one of the most famous images of the Sakyamuni, especially because of the expression of a sublime serenity and compassion. Six human figures kneel at his feet and the halo is decorated with floral scrolls and has two flying celestial figures placed in the corners.

GLOSSARY

Aarti	:	invocation with lights
Aditya	:	aspects of the sun god
Anandavana	:	forest of bliss
Antargriha	:	inner sanctum
Asana	:	seat, position for yoga
Ashram	:	religious retreat
Atman	:	self, spirit or soul
Avatar	:	incarnation of a deity
Avimukta	:	never forsaken
Bhairava	:	terrible aspect of Shiva
Bhakti	:	Hindu devotionalism
Bodhi	:	tree of enlightenment
Bodhisattva	:	a Buddhist saint
Brahmin	:	priestly class
Chaar dhaam	:	four abodes of Vishnu
Chaitya	:	Buddhist prayer hall
Dakshina	:	offering
Darshana	:	viewing the deity
Devalaya	:	temple
Devata	:	god
Devi	:	goddess
Dharma	:	religious law and custom
Dharmachakra	:	wheel of law
Garbha griha	:	sanctum of a temple

Ghats	:	stepped embankments
Guru	:	teacher, saint
Jnana	:	way of knowledge
Jyotirlingam	:	the Shiva lingams of light
Kala	:	time
Karma	:	past actions & their consequences
Kund	:	sacred pool
Iingam	:	phallic symbol of Shiva
Mahasmashana	:	great cremation ground
Mandala	:	sacred & mystical diagrams
Mandapa	:	open pillared hall
Mantra	:	sacred chants
Marta	:	the earth
Matha	:	monastery
Meru	:	mythical mountain
Moksha	:	release from birth & death
Namavali	:	shawl printed with sacred words
Naamkaran	:	naming ceremony
Nagas	:	serpent deities
Nandi	:	Shiva's bull
Nirvana	:	enlightenment
Om	:	sacred syllable
Pitripaksha	:	fortnight when ancestors are worshipped
Pradakshina	:	clockwise circumambulation
Prasad	:	ritual offerings
Prayag	:	confluence of rivers
Prayaschitta	:	atonement
Puja	:	worship of deity
Punya	:	merit
Puranas	:	collection of myths & rituals
Ratha	:	temple chariot
Rishis	:	seers who wrote ancient texts
Rudraksha	:	beads worn by Shiva

GLOSSARY

Sadhu	:	wandering ascetic
Sakyamuni	:	the Buddha
Samsara	:	cycle of birth and death
Sangha	:	Buddhist monastic order
Sannyasin	:	wandering ascetic
Saptapuri	:	seven sacred cities
Shaiva	:	worshipper of Shiva
Shakti	:	divine power of the devi
Shastra	:	ancient treatise
Shloka	:	invocation
Shubha	:	auspicious
Shikhara	:	spire, tower
Shuchi	:	pure
Stupa	:	dome shaped Buddhist shrine
Surya	:	the sun god
Swarga	:	heaven
Swayambhu	:	self created
Tandava	:	Shiva's dance
Tantra	:	esoteric Shaivite sect
Tapas	:	meditation
Tirtha, tirthasthana	:	place of pilgrimage
Tirthayatra	:	pilgrimage
Uttara	:	north
Vaikuntha	:	Vishnu's heaven
Vaishnava	:	worshipper of Vishnu
Vedas	:	oldest Hindu religious text
Vihara	:	Buddhist monastery
Yajna	:	ritual of offerings
Yaksha	:	demigods
Yatra	:	journey
Yoga	:	Indian philosophy
Yogini	:	tantric goddesses

BIBLIOGRAPHY

1. Benaras, The Sacred City – EB Havell
2. Banaras, City of Light – Diana Eck
3. Kashi Ka Itihas (Hindi) – Moti Chandra
4. Varanasi Down the Ages – Kuber Nath Sukul
5. Varanasi Vaibhav (Hindi) – Kuber Nath Sukul
6. Varanasi, The Sacred City of the Hindus – MA Sherring
7. Speaking of Siva – AK Ramanujan
8. The Indian Theogony – Sukumari Bhattacharji
9. Poems of Kabir – (trans.) Rabindra Nath Tagore
10. Kalidasa, The Loom of Time – (trans.) Chandra Rajan
11. The Rig Veda – (trans.) Wendy Doniger O'Flaherty
12. The Dance of Siva – A Coomaraswamy

INDEX

Abhishekha of the lingam, 65
Adi Keshava, 49, 54, 61
Adi Keshava Ghat 2, 6, 9, 53-54, 68, 103
Adi Keshava Temple, 17-18, 26, 54, 67, 85, 112
Adi Manikarnika, 65
Adi Vishweshwara Temple, 55-56, 80-81, 84, 94-95, 113-115
Agni Bindu, 55
Agni puranas, 17
Ahilyabai, Rani, 67
Ahilyabai ghat, 67
Aibak, Qutubuddin, 76, 80, 107-109, 111-114, 136
Aitereya, Brahmana the, 103
Ajatshatru, King, 103, 106-107, 110
akash deep, 54, 100
Akbar, 55-56, 80, 113-114, 138
akharas, 55, 124
Alakananda river, 37
Alam, Shah, 116
Alamgir mosque, 58, 114
Ali, Faujdar Mir, Rustam, 67
Ali, Mir Rustam, 117

Alvar, 115
Amba, 104
Ambalika, 104
Ambika, 104
Anagariha Dharmapala, 138
Anandamoyee, Ma, 110
Annakuta, 100
Annapurna Bhavani, Temple, 83, 86, 100
Annapurna Temple, 49, 63, 117
Anuradhapura, Sri Lanka, 139
Appar, 13
Arjuna, 28
Arthashastra, the, 103
arti
  Bhog, 83
  chanting *mantras,* 82-83
  at Dasashwamedha, 52-53
  garbha griha, 8-9
  Mangala *arti*, 83
  Saptarishi, 83
  Shayan, 83
  Shringar, 83
Ashoka, 39, 75, 103, 107, 111, 135, 137, 139

INDEX

Ashokan pillar sarnath, 137
Ashrams 31, 56, 98, 110
ashvamedha sacrifices, 25-26
Ashvamedha yagna performance of, 50, 112
Asi or Panchganga, 45-46
see also Panchganga
Asi ghat, 25, 47, 49-50, 64, 68, 99
Asi river, 5
Asi sangam ghat, 68
Asi Sangameshwara, 49
Asiatic Society, Calcutta, 137
Assam, 84
Astrology/āstrology learning, 129-131
Aurangzeb, 6, 47, 56-57, 64, 76, 81, 95, 103, 113-114, 124
Avantika (ujjain), 2
see also ujjain
Avimukta, 12
see Kashi Varanasi
Avimukta Mahatmaya, 47-48
Avimukta Vanayaka Temple, 83
Avimukteshwar, 18, 20
Avimukteshwara lingam, 79, 83
Avimukteshwara temple, 7, 83
Ayodhya, 100
Ayurveda centre, 129-130

Badrinath, 37
Bai, Baija, 67, 84
Baji Rao, Peshwa, 51
Bala, 139
Balaki legend about, 110
Bali, 41

Ballabhacharya, 56
Banaras Hindu University (1916) 1941 establishment of, 117
Banarasi *langra* mango, 127
Banarasi *Paan*, 127
Bare Ganesh Temple 85
Basant Panchami, 97
Basavanna, 13-14
Battle of Kurukshetra, 6, 65, 75, 104
Bay of Bengal, 36, 39
Beggers, 8, 51, 120
Besant, Annie, 118
Bhadiani, 47
Bhagavat Gita, the, 34
Bhagirath, King, 35-36, 39
Bhagirathi river, 35, 37
Bhagirath's prayers, 47
Bhairavas, 96
demi-gods, 75
bhairav mythology about, 89-90
bhang, 7, 46, 98, 120, 127
Bharat Mata Temple, 95-96
Bhatta, Narayan, 80, 82, 115
Bhakti, movement, 115
Bhelupura, 111
Bhikshu Bala of Mathura, 138
Bhishma, 104
Bhringi, 28
Bimbisara, 106, 111
Bindu Madhav Temple, 7, 55-58, 67, 80-81, 113, 114, 116
Birlas, 95
Biruni, Al, 103

INDEX **149**

Boatmen temples source of livelihood, 71
Bodh Gaya, 133, 135-136, 139
Bodhi tree, 134, 139
Bodhisattva, 105, 134, 138
Brahma, 13, 18, 20, 22, 24-27, 40-41, 60-61
Brahmanas, 22
Brahmaputra river, 33
Brahmeshwar, 51
Brahmin Kabirs ridiculance, 115
Brihadaranyaka Upanishad, 103
Brihadeshwara Temple, Thanjavur, 29
Brihaspati Temple, 95
Buddha, Gautama (Siddhartha), 6, 45, 75, 103, 106, 109-110, 124, 132-138
Buddhism, 21, 28, 106,
  decline, 136
  patronage during the reign of Ashoka and Kushans,, 135
Buddhist Jataka, 5, 105
Bulls
  beware, 120
Burning ghat, 63

Chait Singh ghat, 66
Chakrapushkarini Kund, 59
  see also manikarnika kund
Chandelas, 107
Chandogya Purana, 103
Chandra, Moti, 111
Chaar Dhams of Badrinath, 4
Charraka, 130

Chaturmasa, 98
Chauhan, Prithviraj, 107,112
Chaukhandi, 138
chaunsath yoginis, 98
Chaunsath Yogini Temple, 67
Chaunsathi Devi Temple, 25
Chaunsathi ghat, 67
Chawki ghat, 67
Chedis, 107
Chellana, 106
Chor ghat, 67
Chunar, 139
Coins of Lalitaditya, 107
Coomaraswamy, Ananda, 29
Cotton texiles, 125,
  weavers contribution, 106
Cows, 8, 120
Craftsman temple source or creativity, 71
Cunnigham, 54
  Alexander, 136-137

Daksha, 22
Dakshina Kashi, 3
Dancers temples source of creativity, 71
Dandapani 83
Dandapani temple, 96
Dasashwamedha, 48-49
  arti at, 52-53
Dasahawamedha arti at, 52-53
Dasashwamedha ghat, 7, 18, 26, 45, 50-52, 63, 68, 96, 98
Dasimayya, Devara, 12

INDEX

Delhi Sultanate, 113
Deva Prayag, 37
Devadeepa Mullika festival, 55
devalayas, 3
Dhameka Stupa, 139
Dhanvantri, 104
dharma disintegration, 27
dharmachakra wheel of law, 139
Dharmachakra Pravartana
  sermon, 111, 133
Dharmarajika Stupa, 137
Dhauli Ganga, 37
Dhundiraja, 85
Dhundiraja, Ganesh, 83
Dhundhiraja Shiva, 85
Divodasa, King 24-31, 50, 75, 88
Divodaseshwara, 27
Diwali or Deepawali, 96, 100
Durga Kund, 87-88
Durga temple, 85, 87-89
Durga Vishalakshi temple, 86
Dussehra, 99
Dwarika (Dwaravati), 2, 4

Eraly, Abraham, 109
Eck, Diana, 59
Elephanta caves Shiva's
  sculptures, 29

Fazl, Abul, 113
Fa Hien Sarnath Visit, 135
Festivals, 50, 55, 61, 85, 87,
  96-101
Four Noble of Truths of
  Buddha, 133

Gabhastishvara temple, 58
Gaghra river, 38
Gahadavala 107, 112, 139
Gai ghat, 67
Gandaka river, 38
Gandhi, Mahatma, 95
Ganesh, Lord, 26-27
  namaskar, to, 71
  as sakshi, 49
Ganesh Chaturthi festival, 85
Ganesh temple of Arka
  Vinayaka, 50, 54
Ganga, 2-3, 8, 11, 15, 26-27,
  54, 86, 89, 103, 105-106,
  108, 115, 122, 133
  ashes immerges after the
    death, 42
  bathing and drinking leads to
    salvation of seven
    generations, 40
  consort of Vishnu and Shiva, 40
  daughter of the Himalayas, 40
  Jagannath woven in braise, 57
  Kalidasa narration in
    Meghadutam, 36
  kinder and gentle, 38-39
  liberation *moksha* to the
    people, 41
  lord Krishna views, 34
  marry Shantanu, 40
  myth of coming to earth 35-36,
    40-41
  never polluted, 41
  numerous names, 41
  symbol of purity, 41

water pouered over the lips
of the dying to ensure
passage to heaven, 41-42
worships and *arati*, 38, 40, 44
Gangadhara, 41, 98
Ganga Lahari, 57, 115
Gangamahal, 47
Ganga Sagar, 36
Gangasagar Mela, 39
Ganga Saptami, 98
Gangotri glacier, 34
Gangotri river, 37
Gangotri temple, 34
ganja, 98
Garhwal Hills, 37
Gaumukh, 34
Gauri Kund, 65
Gaya, 115, 133
Gayatri, 27
Gayatri Mantra, 47
 ghats, 3-6
 built in the 18th and 19th
  centuries, 47
 bhang selling, 46
 boatmen repair their boats, 46
 aratha rulers contribution,
  116-117
 myths, 44-45, 50
 offering handfuls of gangajal
  in praise of Surya, 46-47
 sankalp perform, 48
 spiritual experience of
  pilgrimage, 46
 temples source of livelihood, 71
 washermen drying sarees and
  flapping clothes, 46
 women gossiping, 46
 ghat stairs beware of, 120
Ghazni Mahmund, 6
Ghori, Muhammad, 107, 112
Goddess temples, 72, 83, 86
Golden Temple, 81
Gorakhnathis, 110
Goverdhan, 113, 138
Govindachandra King, 135
 reign, 112
Grant, William James, 89
Gyan Vapi Well (1828), 83-84, 114
Gyan Vapi mosque, 81, 84, 114
Gupta Shiv Prasad, 95

Handicraft, 106, 128
Hanuman image of, 50
Hanuman ghat, 66, 124
Harappan, 16
Haridwar, 4, 39
Harishchandra, King, 67
Harishchandra, ghat, 63, 67
Harivamsa, 17
Harsha of Kanauj, 112
Harshavardhana, 80
Hastings Warren, 66, 81, 103, 117
Hermitages building of, 3
Hindu lunar calendar, 96, 101
Hindu sect, 110, 112
Hinduism, 28, 103
Hiranyakasipu, 28
Holkar Ahilyabai, 81, 117
Holkars, 117
Holi, 96, 98

INDEX

holy man beware of, 120
Hooghly river, 39
Huien Tsang, 5, 80, 103, 112, 135-136

Indian National Congress Varanasi Session of 1904, 117
Indo-Gangetic plains, 135
Indra or Varuna, 15
Indra, Lord, 35
Indus Valley Civilization, 16
Irwin, Lord, 81

Jagannatha, 115
Jahangir, 114
Jahnu, 41
Jai Singh II, Raja, 67
Jaichand, 107, 112
Jain ghat, 66, 111
Jain *tirtha,* 111
Jalasai ghat, 62
Jaleshwar ghat, 63
Janaka, King, 7, 29
Janapadas, 105
Jatar ghat, 67
Jaunpur, 114
Juna Akhara, 66
Jyotishcharya centre of learning, 129
Jyotirlingam, 65, 77, 90,
  numbers, 20
  myth and story, 18-21

Kabir, 6, 45, 56, 70, 93, 103, 115-116

Kabir panthis, 93, 110
Kabir Temple, 93-94
Kabir Chaura, 93
Kabir's *Bijak,* 93
Kailash mountain, 130
Kailasanatha temple, 29
Kal Bhairav, 96
Kal Bhairav temple, 89-91, 114, 117
Kal Kup, 96
Kali Yuga Age, 13
Kalidasa, 10
  Meghadutam poem, 36
Kaliya Daman, 101
Kanchipuram, 2-4, 89
Kanishka, King, 139
Kapalamochan, temple, 20
Kapileshwara, lingam, 83
Kartik Purnima, 55, 100
Kartikeya, 28, 30
Kasa, King, 104
Kashi/Varanasi,
  art and Culture, 117
  centre of India's spiritual soul, 103
  centre of learning, 108, 112
  city of tree sin, 5
  classical dance and music, 125
  classical schools, 110
  commercial centre, 105, 108
  dirty and noisy, with dilapidated buildings, 8
  folk tales of hunters and boatman, 104
  great teachers and scholars, 110

grinding bhang on the ghat steps, 120
gyana worship, 108-110
historical background, 106-108
kachauri Gali, 126
lassi and Thandai drinks, 127
mauj and masti life, 120, 126
mohalla life, 121-124
mythology, worship and rituals, 103-104
religious movement, 103
rivers, 5
social and religious history, 76
speculation about the name, 104-105
sweet shops, 126-127
Thatheri Bazaar, 124
thinkers and teachers role, 103
travellers writings, 103
tirthasthana, 2-9
vegetarian food, 126
wealth of Hindus scholarship preservation, 104
Kashi Karawat temple, 96
Kashi Khanda, 2-3, 48, 59, 63, 64, 77, 84, 88, 103, 115
Kashi ki gali, 121-122, 131
Kashi Rahasya, 77, 86, 103, 115
Kashi Vidya Peeth (1921) establishment of, 118
Kashi Vishwanath temple, 5, 20, 30, 49, 64, 67, 75, 78-83, 86, 94, 117
Katha Upanishad, 48
Kautilya, 103

Kedar meaning, 65
Kedar ghat, 20, 49, 53, 64-66, 79
Kedar temple, 65
Kedareshwar, 18
Kedareshwar temple, 20, 49, 64-65, 78
Kedareshwar temples, 89
Kedarnath, 20
Kedarnath *lingam*, 65
Kedarnath temple, 29
Khalji, Alauddin, 6
Kharva Vinayaka, temple, 54, 85
Khatri, Durga Prasad, 95
Kites flying, 46
Koshala, 106, 108, 138
Kosetsu Nosu, 139
Krishna, Lord, 34
Krishna Leela, 100
Krishnamurthy, J., 118
Krittivas temple, 114
Kroshas, 60-61
Kshatriyas, 110
Kubereshwara, *lingam*, 83
Kumaradevi, 135
Kurma, 17
Kurus, 40
Kushars, 135, 139
Kushinagar, Buddha gained *nirvana*, 135

Lakshmidhara, 89, 112
Lakulisa, 121
Lal Darwaza mosque, 114
Lal, Lala Kashmiri, 63
Lat Bhairav, 99

INDEX

Lalita Devi temple, 67
Lalita ghat, 67
Linga, 17
Linga Purana, 62
Lingams, 27
  numbers, 78
Linayat, 21
Lodi, Sikander, 80, 114
Lolarka Kund, 25, 49, 98
Lolarka Shashthi, 99
Lumbini, birth place of Buddha, 135
Luxor, 6

Macaulay, 128
Madhavacharya, 110
Magadha, 105-107, 135
Mahabharata, the, 5, 17, 40, 104
Mahabharata war, 6
Mahadeva temple, 114
Mahakala *lingam,* 83
Maharaja of Vijianagram, 64
Mahavagga, the, 105
Mahavira, Vardhaman, 103, 109, 111
Makar Sankranti, 50, 97
Malaviya, Pandit Madan Mohan, 94, 117
Malaviya Bridge, 53, 67, 106
Man Mandir ghat, 67, 113
Mandakini river, 37
mandapas, 80
mandapas series, 79
Mandhatri, 65
Mangala Gauri Temple, 56, 58

Manikarni Devi worship of, 62
Manikarikeshwara temple, 62
Manikarnika, 47-49, 54
Manikarnika Ghat, 17, 58-64, 82, 85
Manikarnika bathes, 82
Manikarnika Kund, 59, 62
Mansaram, Pandit, 117
Mansarovar ghat, 67, 113
Manusmiriti, 103
Mata Anandmayee ghat, 66
Mathas, 110
Mathura, 2, 4
Matsya, 17
Mauni Amavasya, 50
Maya (Haridwar), 2
  see also Haridwar
Mayukhaditya temple, 58
Megasthenes, 103
Mimamsa, school, 110
Mir ghat, 27, 67
moksha, 2, 41, 130
Mokshavilas temple, 80
Monkeys beware of, 120, 122
Monasteries, 110-111
Mount Kailash, 11, 15
Mount Mandara, 24-26
Mount Meru, 27
Mulagandhakuti Vihara, 138-139
Mulagandhakuti shrine, 138
Mundaka Upanishad, 109
mundan ceremony, 52
Muni, Kapil, 35
Musicians temple source of creativity to, 71

INDEX 155

Nag Nathiya celebration, 100-101
Naga Panchami festival, 61
Nagar Junakonda, 138
Nagwa ghats, 68
namkaran puja ceremony, 52
Nanak, Guru, 6, 45, 103
Nandakini river, 37
Nandi bull, 15, 28, 72, 81, 83
Natya Shastra, 18
Nava Durga, 78
Nava Gauries, 78
Navaratra. 99
Nayanmar, 13
Neema, 93
Neeru, 93
New Vishwanath Temple, 94-95
Nikumbheshwara *lingam*, 83
Nilkantheshwara *lingam*, 83
Nineveh, 6
Nishadh ghats, 66
Nishadhraj ghat, 65
Nishbama Yatra, 48

Omkareshwara, 78
Omkareshwar temple, 7, 20, 79, 114

Paan shops, 120, 130
Padmeshwara temple, 114
Paduka Tirtha, 26
Painters, temples source of creativity to, 71
Palas, 107
Panch Kroshi, *Yatra*, 54
Panchganga, 47, 49, 54, 56

Panchganga Ghat, 27, 54-58, 64, 93, 96, 100
Panchtirthi yatra, 47-49, 54, 62-63
Pandas, 51, 71, 120
Pandava, 6, 65
Parashuram, 29
Parshvanatha, Lord, 6, 111
Parvati, 3, 11, 24, 27-28
Pasupati, 20-21, 31
Patalipurta, 39, 135
Patanjali, 103, 110
Peshwas, 117
Pindadaan ceremony, 52
Pitripaksha, 99
Prabhu, Allama, 14
Prasenajit, King, 106-107
Prathiharas, 107
Prayag, 37, 115
Prayag ghat, 68
prayashitta rituals, 6
Purna kumbha, 40
Punyakriti, 26
Puranas, the, 5, 85, 104-105, 115
Puri, 4
Pururavas dynasty, 104
Pushyamitra Sunga, 112

Raj ghat, 67
Rajabhallabh ghat, 63
Rajagriha, 108
Rajendra Prasad ghat, 67
Rajghat Plateau, 53, 106-107
Ram Bharat Milap, 99
Ram Leela, 99-100

INDEX

Ram! Ram muttering, 56
Rama, Lord, 6, 17, 29, 35, 99-100
Ram ghats, 66
Ramananda, Swami, 56, 93, 115
Ramanuja, 103, 110
Ramayana, the, 5, 17, 92, 99, 116
Ramcharitmanas, the, 50, 92, 116
Rameshwaram, 4, 17, 20
Rameshwaram Temple, 29
Rani Bhawani, 87
Rangbhari Ekadashi, 97-98
Rao, Peshwa Baji,
Rao, Sadashiv, 117
Rashtrakutas, 107
Ravana, 6, 17, 28
Razia Sultan, 76, 80, 114
Relics of the Buddha, 138
Religion good business, 8
Rickshawallas telling myth about Shiva, 9
Temples source of livelihood, 71
Rig Veda, the, 15, 103
Ripunjaya, King, 24
Rishikesh, 38
Rishipattana, 111, 133
see also, sarnath
Rudra, 15, 84
rudraksha beads, 7, 11, 15, 131
Rudra Prayag, 37
Rudravasa, 5, 12, 16
see, Kashi-Varanasi

Sadhus, 122
Safdarjung, Nawab, 63
Sagara, King, 35
Sakshi Vinayaka Temple, 49, 63, 85, 117
Sambandar, 13-14
Sammitiya School, 136
Sanchi *Stupa* at, 136-137
Sangha, Buddhist monastic order, 134
Sangameshwara, *lingam,* 54
Sangameshara temple, 54
Sankat Mochan Temple, 91
Sankata Devi Temple, 86
Sankatha ghat, 65
Sankhya School, 110
Sanskrit College, 117
Sanskrit *shlokas* reciting of, 8
Sapta Samudri, Tirtha, 37
Saraswati, 39, 54
   Buddha's sermons to five bhikshus, 106
   centre of Buddhism's, 135
   deer park Mrigadaya, 134
   golden figure of Buddha, 136
   Hiuen Tsang, description, 136
   monasteries, 135
   pilgrimage place, 28
   Qutubuddin Aibak invasion and burning monasteries, 136
   rishis and the *sadhus* for meditation, 134
   Stupas, 75, 112, 135-138
   Viharas repairing and building new, 135
Sarnath Museum account, 139-140
Satapatha Brahmana, 103

Sati, 22-23
Saubhagya Gauri, 83
Savitri, 83
Shah, Mahammad, 117
Shahjahan, 113-15
Shaivas sects, 13, 21
Shakta, 29
Shankaracharya, Adi, 4, 6, 9, 103, 110
Shankaracharya of Shringeri, 87
Sharqi Nawabs, 76, 114
Sherring, M.A., 6
Shikoh, Dara, 113
Shitala Temple, 51, 86, 95
Shiva, Lord, 4, 11, 17
  and King Divodasa, 24-31
  bhang favourite drink, 46
  Daksha's sacrifice, 22-24
  Damaru, Trishula and a begging bowl, 15, 29
  five faces, 20, 30
  flag with the bull emblem, 27
  generous with his boons, 28
  gyana Dakshinamurti, 30
  myth about, 9, 17-18
  myths about unique garments, 21
  numerous names, 16-18, 20-21, 28-29, 31, 59, 129-130
  snakes writhe around his neck, 15, 21
  rudraksha beads in his neck, 15
  tandava dance, 7, 13, 29-30, 97
  worship, 12-14
Shiva Purana, 60

Shiva Temple, 18, 72-73, 75
Shivaji, Chhatrapati, 116
Shivakeshi, 3
Shivala ghat, 117
Shivalingam, 12-14, 18-19, 71, 77, 80
Shivaratri, 30-31, 83, 92, 97
  Sharddha funeral rites of, 42, 99
  shringara ceremonies, 62, 97
Shuddhodhana, King 124
Shukla Paksha, of *Kartik* festival, 87
Shulatankeshwar, 51
Siddhi Vinayaka, 85
Siddhi, Vinayaka Temple, 63
Silk, 124, 128-129
Singers temples source of creativity, 71
Singh, Balwant, 66
Singh, Chet, 117
Singh, Jagat, 137
Singh, Raja Man 113-114
Singh, Maharaja Ranjit, 81
Sindhia, Daulat Rao, 67, 84
Sindhia, Mahadji, 116
Sindhia ghat, 67
Sindhias, 117
Sir-i-Akbar, 113
Sita, 17, 29, 50
Skanda, 17
Skanda Purana, 3
Sri Lanka, 139
Sukul, Kubernath, 63
Sundarar, 13

158 INDEX

Suri, Prabha, 111
Svetasvatara Upanishad, 16
Surya Temple, 58
Sursuta, 130
swayambhu, 77, 82
swayambhu lingam, 65

Tagore, Rabindranath, 94
Tailangaswami, 56
Tara mantra singing of, 62
Taraka Mantra, 4
Tarakeshwara Temple, 62
Tarpana ceremony, 52, 99
Tavernier, Jean Baptist, 5, 56
  destruction during the mughal
    period, 6-7, 76, 80-81, 108,
    113
  arti lamp, 73
  Chola King contribution, 29
  Chanting of the *swagata,* 74
  during the Gupta period 112
  intones 'Om Shanti' 73-74
  maratha rulers role in
    building, 76, 116-117
  myths, 18
  numbers, 63, 112
  Pallava Kings contribution, 29
  puja ceremony, 72-73
  rituals, 72
Temples source of livelihood, 71
Textile trade centre, 128, 138
Thandai drinks, 98
Tibet Buddhism in, 21
tirthasthana, 2-9, 20
Tirthavivechana kanda, 112

Todarmal, Raja, 55, 80, 95,
  113, 115, 138
Trilochana temple, 117
Tripundraka, 15
Tripurantaka, 30
Triveni, 39
Triveni Sangam of Allahabad, 37
Tughlak, Firuz Shah, 80, 114
Tulsi, 47
Tulsi Ghat, 44
Tulsi Manas Temple, 92
Tulsidas, 6, 45, 56, 91-92, 99,
  103, 116
Touristguides temple source of
  livelihood, 71
Tyre, 6

Ujjain, 4
Upanayan ceremony, 52
Upanishads, the, 109, 130

Vaisheshika school, 110
Vajira, 107
Vallabhacharya, Swami, 66, 110
Varanasi school of Ayurveda,
  130
Varanasi Vaibhav, 63
Varuna river, 5, 26, 54, 106
Varuna sangam, 48, 54, 64
Vedas, the, 19, 104, 109
vihara temple, 135
vihara, 134, 135
Vichitravirya, 104
Vira Shaivas, 21, 110
Virupaksha Gauri, 83

INDEX

Vishalakshi temple, 78
Vishnu, 13, 15, 17-19, 26-27, 30, 35, 54, 59-60
Vishnu Prayag, 37
Vishnu Temple, 72
Vishwanath, Lord, 81
Vishwanath Gali, 49, 63, 79, 85-86, 95, 123, 126, 130
Vishwanatha *lingam*, 79, 84
Vishweshwar, lord, 13, 18, 20, 64, 78
Vishweshwar, *lingam*, 67, 81
Vishweshwar temple, 7, 64, 89, 124
Vivekananda, Swami, 110

Weavers, 123
Weavers contribution, 106
Weavers living area, 129
Weavers temple source of livelihood, 71
Weavers weaving the silk for the deities and priests, 71
Weaving industry, 128
Widows, beware of, 120

Yakshas, 21, 96
Yamuna river, 27, 37, 39, 54
Yasa (Buddha's first disciple), 106, 125, 134
Yoga learning centre, 129-130
Yoga school, 110
Yoginis, 25, 27-28, 67, 75, 96
Yotishcharya, 131
Yudhishthira, 29